**LOHFELD
CONSULTING
GROUP, INC.**

Lohfeld Consulting Group

Insights

Volume 2

Capture & Proposal
Insights & Tips

Edited by Beth Wingate

Lohfeld Consulting Group

Insights

Capture & Proposal
Insights & Tips

Edited by Beth Wingate

Published by Lohfeld Consulting Group, Inc.
940 South River Landing Road
Edgewater, Maryland 21037

For more information, contact BWingate@LohfeldConsulting.com

Production, Design, and Copyediting: Alexandra Wingate

| Dedication

We dedicate this second Insights book to our families, whose daily support enables us to do what we love best, and to our colleagues, whose positive reviews of our first book and added encouragement compelled us to share more insights and tips with our capture and proposal community.

Insights

Capture & Proposal Insights and Tips – Volume 2

Contents

Insights

Capture & Proposal Insights and Tips – Volume 2

Insights

Capture & Proposal Insights and Tips – Volume 2

Insights

Capture & Proposal Insights and Tips – Volume 2

Insights

Capture & Proposal Insights and Tips – Volume 2

Insights

Capture & Proposal Insights and Tips – Volume 2

Insights
Capture & Proposal Insights and Tips – Volume 2

Capture

Insights

The 25% solution

Brenda Crist

I titled this the *25% solution* because proposal managers often have little more than 25% of the solution completed before the request for proposal (RFP) drops. According to best practices, by the time the RFP drops, a company should have:

- An established relationship with the client or at least a dialogue with the client

- A solution for performing the work or at least a concept of operations (CONOPS)

- A price-to-win (PTW) strategy or at least an idea of the customer's budget

- Knowledge of the competition's solution, PTW, or organizational capabilities

- Partners in place to help close solution gaps with signed non-disclosure agreements (NDA)

- Subject matter experts (SME) available and willing to help craft the solution

When given a 25% solution, the proposal manager becomes a defacto capture manager because once the RFP drops the original capture manager is usually consumed with completing the pricing and contract documents and serving as the liaison between company executives and subcontractors. As a result of the time crunch, the proposal manager is often left to:

- Oversee development of the solution and ensure it provides sufficient detail
- Perform competitive analyses to resolve open questions
- Design the transition plan and identify transition risks
- Develop the quality control (QC) plan or operations-monitoring approach
- Oversee recruiting of key personnel
- Identify benefits and discriminators and develop win themes

At this point, you're probably thinking, "Shouldn't the company no bid?" While this is often the case, there are many compelling reasons to bid including:

- The company had a surge in operational work
- The company's budget was cut

Insights
Capture & Proposal Insights and Tips – Volume 2

- Multiple bids came out at the same time

No matter the reason, it becomes the proposal manager's job to complete the unfinished capture work and develop the proposal within the timeframe allocated by the customer. So how can the proposal manager possibly perform all these functions within the customer's timeframe? Here are my recommendations:

- Quickly construct a compliance matrix and assess the work that needs to be completed

- Identify if there is reasonable cause to ask for an extension, and if so, request one

- Build a schedule that maximizes parallel tasks and minimizes sequential tasks

- Allocate 15% to 33% of the proposal response timeframe to completing capture activities including the competitive analysis, technical and management solution development, and key personnel recruitment tasks

- As soon as the schedule is completed, communicate resource needs to top executives along with associated risks if the resource requirements are not met

- Immediately after the Kick-Off Meeting, convene a working session to develop the technical, management, and staffing solution within the parameters of the PTW estimate

- Before 33% of the proposal timeframe is spent, review the solution with upper management and mitigate risks

- Before 66% of the proposal time is spent, conduct rolling reviews of annotated outlines for all proposal sections

- Aim for a final review of the proposal before 80% of the proposal timeframe is completed, and limit the number of proposal reviewers to allow sufficient time to incorporate their feedback

- Always allocate the final 10% of your timeframe to a quality review of the proposal and production

In summary, the *25% solution* is becoming more of the norm these days as companies reduce their overhead costs and proposal professionals are asked to do more with less. The situation is becoming more feasible as customers invite more questions and input during the solicitation timeframe and proposal due dates slide to the right. The situation becomes more palatable if upper management supports a scalable, flexible, and adaptable proposal management process.

Bold trends in capture and proposal management Q&A

Bob Lohfeld

During Bob Lohfeld's *Bold trends in capture and proposal management* webinar, part of the Lohfeld Business Winning Webinar Series, Bob presented some of the more interesting trends in capture and proposal management and discussed how these are changing the competitive landscape for companies looking to increase their win probabilities.

Bob answered a number of questions for webinar participants during and after the webinar. Here are some of the questions and Bob's answers.

Q: With respect to testing our proposed solutions with the customer to obtain feedback, how do you deal with contracting offices that do not allow interaction in advance of even a draft RFP?

A: You want to validate your assumptions and test your solution with the customer before locking these down. If you are pre-RFP and the contracting officer won't allow discussions, then that individual is doing you an injustice, and hopefully you can use the myth busting memos to open up communications. These memos were written by the heads of the Office of Federal Procurement Policy (OFPP) to deal with exactly the issue you raise.

Myth-Busting 1 Memo Feb. 2011
(http://goo.gl/VJs5LN)

Myth-Busting 2 Memo May 2012
(http://goo.gl/cBmhqC)

If none of this works, then find a surrogate for your customer. Use a former government employee or consultant. Try a subcontractor who might become a team member. There are lots of options. The important thing to remember is you don't want to base your entire proposal on assumptions that are untested and a solution that may end up being what you want to offer, but not what your customer wants to buy.

Watch the webinar replay and download Bob's presentation (http://goo.gl/NGG4pK)

Insights
Capture & Proposal Insights and Tips – Volume 2

Q: With reduced government budgets, do you foresee a continuation or rise in the number of lowest price technically acceptable (LPTA) type bids?

A: I think we will see fewer LPTA procurements used in the services side of the business—even with declining budgets—because these are bad for the government for lots of reason.

Here are some articles that I wrote in Washington Technology that discuss some of these negative features.

Lohfeld Consulting Group Articles – 5 questions to derail LPTA (http://goo.gl/iNsVM1)

Lohfeld Consulting Group Articles – Will LPTA make us all losers (http://goo.gl/NX83wj)

Lohfeld Consulting Group Articles – Why some companies embrace LPTA (http://goo.gl/FiwLqZ)

Lohfeld Consulting Group Articles – Is the government starting to hate LPTA too (http://goo.gl/1JPXVq)

Additionally, both Frank Kendall (DOD) and Joe Jordan (OFPP) are encouraging agencies to narrow the use of LPTA bids to just those bid that are for commodity purchases.

Insights
Capture & Proposal Insights and Tips – Volume 2

The pendulum is swinging away from LPTA bids, but this is just my opinion, and we'll have to wait to know for sure what happens to LPTA.

Q: Using the dashboard in slide #9, how are you creating a score, and how is the score being validated? I see a number, but what created that score?

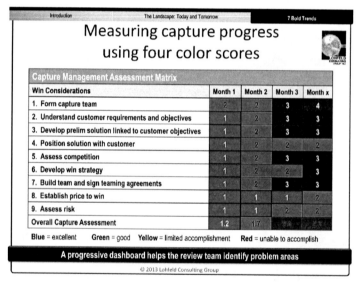

A: You can use numbers instead of colors to assess how well each activity is performed. Don't make the math too complicated. You can equate a numerical rating of four to a blue score, three to a green score, and so on.

Personally, I prefer the color scores because people will tend to rig the numerical scores to get the rating that they want. With the color scores, I ask them to justify why they chose that color and then listen to the explanation to see if it has merit.

Some of our more sophisticated clients have independent organizations that validate the assessments. For example, if you have an organization that does competitive assessments, then they can review the competitive assessment for a particular procurement and offer a professional opinion about the quality of the work that was done.

I don't think you have to be too precise in this exercise, and notional scores will help you achieve what you want, which is to stop funding programs that are losers and help draw management attention to areas where your capture team needs assistance. If you can do that, your dashboards will be pretty effective.

Q: There are still many agencies focused on LPTA. What are your thoughts on how to compete in an LPTA environment?

A: Focus the government on establishing technical acceptability. If they fail to define technical acceptability, then the procurement will be a pricing race into the abyss.

Insights
Capture & Proposal Insights and Tips – Volume 2

If you can establish an acceptable technical floor, this will help prevent bidders from offering unreasonably low prices. If you can't accomplish this, then it's time for difficult decision-making.

If you're not going to be the lowest bidder, then there is no point in bidding. Back away from those jobs that you cannot win, and save your money for procurements that are better suited to your company.

Q: We have capture steps/process that we follow (which probably most other companies have), and we tally the wins/losses/cancelled, but the analytics is what we lack.

A: Your analytics don't have to be very complex to begin getting meaningful data about your organization and begin optimizing your process. If you make up a balanced score card (see slide #9) to color score the attributes of a good procurement to pursue and use that, you will begin to see that sound pursuit decisions generally result in a win.

You will also see that there are some managers who bid and lose almost every time, and there are others who win more often than not. These managers are just making better pursuit decisions.

Start your analytics by keeping it simple and you'll be amazed at what you can learn.

Q: In an LPTA competition, how is the capture process applied when most of the process is now involved with pricing strategy first and technical as a secondary qualifier?

A: This really needs to be a discussion. I would tell you the process should be the same for LPTA and other best-value procurements. How you apply what you learn carrying out the capture process is different, but the steps in capture are the same.

Insights

Capture & Proposal Insights and Tips – Volume 2

Proposal Production

Insights

Proposal production across the business development life cycle—Part 1: What is production?

Briana Coleman

Think about how you got to work today. You probably drove a car, took a train, or caught a bus. That's the simple version of the story. In reality, the car, the train, and the bus companies spent hundreds of hours using thousands of people to assemble your final transportation vessel.

This is what we call *production.*

Each end product started with a small team of technical minds who conceptualized, designed, and engineered it. Then they turned the plan over to the thousands who work on the production process—a production process using the assembly line pioneered in 1908. It's a process that requires thousands of workers to produce a car, a train, a thing…anything. This production process is still used today as a matter of best practice to ensure consistent, perfect products every time.

From the industrial revolution until today, manufacturers of goods have placed great emphasis on the production process because they know that even the greatest idea is no good if they fail to bring that product to market in an attractive package that consumers want to buy.

In proposal-land, our final books and CDs are the products of our labor. They are what the evaluators see and judge us on. But do we adopt the production best practices from every other industry?

Let's see…a typical proposal looks something like this: we spend months thinking about our solution. We pull in every bright mind—and sometimes not so bright mind—we know to help us think. These huge teams critique us at Blue Team, Pink Team, Red Team, Gold Team, Gold Team 2, *for real this time, final Gold Team*. They tweak each word until it sings a perfect melody from the page.

But by now, we are 24 hours from due date. The development team breathes a huge sigh of relief for a job well done and tosses the proposal over the cubicle wall to *Production*. Production is a mysterious land of wonder that routinely makes magic happen, despite the 24 hours they have to edit, desktop publish, check for compliance, print, assemble, and deliver a winning product, all with one or two people, because after all, the rest of the team is on to another proposal.

Hmmm…sounds like the exact opposite of the best practices used to produce every other product we touch!

Through this six-part series, I'm going to discuss the importance of production in the proposal life cycle. I'll share some of my war stories to illustrate this single, very important point:

Even the best proposal is only as good as its execution.

Contractors fight many battles during the war to win business with the government, from capture management, to solutioning, to finding key personnel. You can win all of these battles but still lose the war if you don't succeed on the final task—producing and delivering the bid!

Proposal production across the business development life cycle—Part 2: Intro to the life cycle

Briana Coleman

What is *production*? Many people in our industry think of production as simply printing and assembling our proposals. But, production also includes all of the steps that lead up to our ability to hit *Print*. These include desktop publishing, graphic design, and editing—all necessary before you print and assemble your books, and most importantly, deliver your winning proposal!

These activities are typically thought of as tasks we accomplish in the last few days before delivery; however, I want to impress upon you that production activities should be incorporated throughout your business development (BD) life cycle.

Insights
Capture & Proposal Insights and Tips – Volume 2

The graphic below depicts a typical BD life cycle with five phases:

- Phase 1 Opportunity identification and assessment

- Phase 2 Pursuit

- Phase 3 Pre-proposal preparation

- Phase 4 Proposal development

- Phase 5 Post-submittal

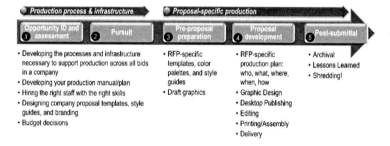

While we're all familiar with how proposal management fits into the overall BD life cycle, I want to discuss how production fits into the life cycle. The high-level production activities for each phase are discussed below; I'll dive deeper into each phase in later posts.

Phase 1 Opportunity identification and assessment and Phase 2 Pursuit

Remember, these are the activities you should be performing before you ever have a real proposal on your plate. Two main activities should be accomplished in this phase:

- Document your production plan
- Develop company templates

Phase 3 Pre-proposal preparation

- Begin drafting your production plan—proposal-specific
- Revise templates to meet (anticipated) RFP requirements—fonts, size, colors, etc.
- Begin conceptualizing graphics
- Revise style guides to meet client-specific naming conventions/acronyms

Phase 4 Proposal development

- Implement production plan

Phase 5 Post-submittal

- Archive and shred!
- Conduct lessons learned activities

Insights

Proposal production across the business development life cycle—Part 3: Phases 1 and 2

Briana Coleman

In my previous section, I outlined a typical business development life cycle with five phases:

- Phase 1 Opportunity identification and assessment

- Phase 2 Pursuit

- Phase 3 Pre-proposal preparation

- Phase 4 Proposal development

- Phase 5 Post-submittal

In this section, I'll discuss the key production activities you should perform in Phases 1 and 2.

Remember, these are the activities you should be performing **before** you ever have a real proposal on your plate. There are two main activities that you should accomplish in this phase.

1. Document your production plan

Your production war plan is not something to be written in an afternoon and put on a shelf. It requires numerous trade-off assessments, decisions, and training of staff when it is complete.

The goal of the production plan is to ensure that you have thought through all elements of production—desktop publishing, editing, graphics, printing, and delivery—and determined how your company will accomplish each of these.

As you make decisions, always keep in mind this goal—eliminate single points of failure! This means that you should have a backup plan for every step in your production. For example, don't rely on a single desktop publisher to do all proposals or a single printer. Always ask yourself, "What could go wrong with this plan?" and then develop a contingency plan for that potential point of failure.

So what goes into your production war plan?

Who will perform? Identify all of the positions that will have a hand in your proposal production, and ensure that you have multiple resources identified for each. Remember, even if you have a primary desktop publisher/graphic artist, etc., develop relationships with secondary resources that you can call on when you're in a jam. People get sick, hurt, or quit—so don't rely on one person!

Software decisions. How will desktop publishing be done? Will you use MS Word, Adobe InDesign, or something else? What about graphics? What version of software do you need? Does everyone need to have the latest version or only the production team? How will this affect your document-sharing procedures? Consider the pros and cons of each software platform, the users and skills you have at your disposal, and your budget. Make a decision, and then ensure that your assigned resources are experts in the software—or train them until they are!

Version control and archiving. Are you going to use software like WinCenter™, SharePoint, or Privia, or are you going to use email and network folders? Develop guidelines for sharing documents, updating documents, and maintaining version control. Consider who will be ultimately responsible for maintaining a master file—is it your desktop publisher or your proposal manager? How will you ensure that you incorporate changes from multiple sources without compromising version control? How will you archive old versions and name final versions? Who will be responsible for this?

Printing and assembly. This is a **huge** decision. It includes how you will print (internal versus external), what type of printers and paper you will use, printer settings, how you will do tabs, how you will print covers and spines, will you print full bleed or not, labels for boxes, CD labels and how they will be printed, etc.

Style guides. A style guide documents your editing preferences. What standards will you follow? What are your punctuation preferences, spelling guides, etc.?

Templates and corporate branding. This section is discussed in detail below.

Staffing Decisions. Production roles are not mutually exclusive. Many graphic artists can also desktop publish, and many proposal managers serve as the production manager, etc. Determine how many people you need based on the size, complexity, and turnaround time of your proposals. For a 2-week task order response, don't expect your proposal manager to have the time to do everything; for longer responses, you may be able to double dip on duties.

2. Develop company templates

Design, develop, and agree to your company templates. These templates will change with each proposal, but hopefully it will be a matter of tweaking and not developing from scratch.

When you develop templates, consider how you could tailor each to be client specific—perhaps creating placeholders for graphics or images that could be swapped in and out for each cover or a placeholder for a logo in the header or footer.

Ensure you have templates for:

- Paragraph styles/headings
- Headers and footers
- Title pages
- Covers/spines
- Tables/charts

By developing your production plan and company templates, you will prevent your company from reinventing the wheel every time you work on a new proposal!

Proposal production across the business development life cycle—Part 4: Phase 3

Briana Coleman

Here are the key production activities that you should perform in Phase 3 Pre-Proposal Preparation.

1. Begin drafting your production plan: proposal-specific

In Phases 1 and 2 of the BD life cycle, you drafted a company production plan. In this phase, you'll tailor that generic plan to your specific proposal and RFP.

By this phase in the life cycle, you have likely received a draft RFP from the client, or you have put together a strawman RFP of your anticipated requirements. Using these draft documents, update your plan to reflect any nuances of the customer, e.g., specified font sizes, paper requirements (e.g., 100% recycled), delivery issues (e.g., must use FedEx), graphic restrictions, etc.

2. Revise templates to meet (anticipated) RFP requirements

In accordance with your proposal-specific production plan, update your company templates to match the anticipated RFP requirements. Ensure that your fonts, font sizes, margins, header/footers, and other formatting are in compliance with the draft/strawman RFP.

3. Begin conceptualizing graphics

Develop and solidify your proposal-specific color palette, considering the client and their preferences in your color choices.

Separately from your production plan, your proposal manager has probably begun working with the writers by this point. The writers are beginning to develop storyboards or annotated outlines and documenting the solution. Engage your graphic artists early, and have them begin working with your writers to conceptualize draft graphics. Note that I am not saying *render*. Graphics rarely hit the mark on the first try, and they are expensive to render. Instead, have your graphic artists spend their time directing questions to the authors, presenting ideas, and sketching rough graphics that will be rendered after Pink Team.

4. Revise style guides to meet client-specific naming conventions/acronyms

Update your company's standard style guide to create a proposal-specific guide for use by writers, editors, and the proposal manager once the RFP drops. Include client- or industry-specific acronyms, how you will refer to the client (e.g., U.S. Department of Defense vs. DOD), words or phrases to avoid, etc.

By developing your proposal-specific production plan and updating templates ahead of time, you will ensure that you are ready to hit the ground running when the RFP arrives!

Insights

Capture & Proposal Insights and Tips – Volume 2

Proposal production across the business development life cycle—Part 5: Phase 4

Briana Coleman

Once you receive your final RFP, you can begin actually implementing your production plan. Below is a typical 30-day schedule to give you a sense of when you should begin each element of production. You'll note that final production begins on DAY 1!

SUNDAY	MONDAY	TUESDAY	WEDNESDAY	THURSDAY	FRIDAY	SATURDAY
	1 **RFP Released** DETERMINE FORMAT/DELIVERY REQT'S	2 REFINE TEMPLATE/SHELLS DESIGN COVERS	3 **Kick-off** DESIGN COVER CONFIRM SIGNER'S AVAILABILITY	4 DESIGN COVERS CONCEPTUALIZE GRAPHICS	5 COVER DRAFT 1 DUE CONCEPTUALIZE GRAPHICS	6
7	8 SCHEDULE PRINTER OR PRODUCTION FACILITY CONCEPTUALIZE GRAPHICS	9 FINAL COVER DESIGNED CONCEPTUALIZE GRAPHICS	10 Pink Team DESIGN TITLE PAGE & HEADERS; RENDER GRAPHICS	11 DESIGN TITLE PAGE & HEADERS; RENDER GRAPHICS	12 DESIGN TITLE PAGE & HEADERS; RENDER GRAPHICS PREPARE PRODUCTION CHECKLIST	13
14	15 FINAL TITLE PAGE, HEADERS, GRAPHICS	16 DESKTOP PUBLISH PRINT BOOKS	17 Red Team	18 *Refine Graphics* ORDER SUPPLIES	19 *Refine Graphics*	20
21	22 *Final Graphics* FINAL EDITING	23 FINAL EDITING FINAL DP	24 FINAL DP PRINT BOOKS	25 Gold Team: Morning PRODUCTION	26 PRODUCTION OVERNIGHT MAIL	27
28	29 DELIVERY	30 **Proposal DUE**				

By Day 2, you should be able to refine your templates to match the format/delivery requirements of your RFP. Note that I am saying *refine*, and not *develop*, because you will have already taken care of baseline templates in your pre-proposal phase. Here, you'll update fonts and font sizes and develop shells. Shells are MS Word documents containing all of your paragraph styles, headers, and footers—with the actual headings and RFP instructions embedded in the document.

Use the first week to design your cover as well. Your production plan may dictate a standard cover that you will use; however, even standard covers should be able to be tailored to each client. Use this first week to design or tweak the cover—and have it ready for review at Pink Team. Once you get approval at Pink Team, you can design or refine your spines, title pages, headers, footers, and CD labels to coordinate with the main cover.

Work on graphic conceptualization in the first week, after you've assigned sections to authors at kick-off. **Stop spending money on rendering graphics until they are fully conceptualized and vetted!** Spend time up front actually conceptualizing the graphics and vetting them in Pink Team. Only after the graphics are vetted and authors have received content suggestions in Pink Team should you take the time to render your graphics.

By the beginning of week 2, schedule your printer and production facility. If you are using an outside printer, ensure that they are available on your selected printing days—and get yourself on their calendars early. This will ensure you are a priority for them when the job comes around. If you are printing in-house, ensure that the company as a whole knows when you intend to print. This is particularly important for larger corporations with multiple proposal teams that may be fighting for valuable resources simultaneously.

By week 3, you can begin desktop publishing your proposal. I always save a full day before Red Team to rough desktop publish the books. It can be distracting to desktop publish for Pink Team— you want people to worry about content in Pink Team, and having desktop published Pink Team volumes helps reviewers concentrate on the content. But by Red Team, you need to ensure that you are within page count, the design doesn't offend anybody on the review panel, and the direction is the right one.

Post-Red Team, you are really only giving a couple of days to your authors to fix whatever needs changing prior to Gold Team. Post-Red Team is not the time to completely rewrite your proposal. Instead, have the authors work with the graphic artists to finalize the graphics, get their content within page count, and ensure compliance.

Now comes the controversial part of the schedule—the part that usually is left to the last 24 hours before a proposal is due, if it's done at all— the final editing and desktop publishing.

Assuming you have different people doing editing and desktop publishing, start with editing. Give your editor a full 1.5 days to edit the entire proposal—all volumes, covers, footers, everything. You may have to allow for even more time depending on the size of the proposal. As each section is edited, release that section to the desktop publisher.

Desktop publishing is where you make every page sing and the content pop. Ideally, the editor and desktop publisher should work closely together— because you may find yourself slightly over page count after desktop publishing. A good desktop publisher has tricks to get extra lines on a page, while a good editor can recommend words to cut if the page limits aren't perfect at the end.

You'll notice that after Gold Team, we are leaving 2 days for printing and assembly. We are also delivering the proposal overnight **2 days** before it's due. Government offices often have very lengthy processes for receiving packages, and proposals have been known to get stuck in the mailroom for a day.

When you put your actual proposal schedule together, keep in mind these facts about how long each production element takes and how much it will cost if you use outside help.

Production Budgets & Timelines

Production Element	Average Timeframe	Average Direct Costs
Graphic Development	• 1-2 hours for simple graphics • 6-8 hours for complex graphics • 8 hours+ for complex illustrations	Consultant: $90-$120/hour
Desktop Publishing	8 pages/hour for page layout	Consultant: $125-$150/hour
Word Templates	4-6 hours (creation)	Consultant: $125-$150/hour
Editing	5 pages/hour	Consultant: $125-$150/hour
Printing	•Internal: 1 page/minute •External: 1,000 pages/hour (fully printed and assembled)	•Internal: $.10-$.20/color page + labor and materials •External: $.65-$.85/color page
White Glove Review (Book Check)	2-4 hours	N/A

While we all think about when to schedule Red Team and how long an author needs to write, we often forget about production details when putting together our master schedule. Use these tips, and you'll find yourself well-prepared when delivery day comes around!

Proposal production across the business development life cycle—Part 6: Phase 5

Briana Coleman

Now I'll discuss the key production activities that you should perform in the final phase—Phase 5 Post-submittal.

1. Archive and shred!

The production life cycle creates a lot of artifacts—both electronic and hard copy. Don't forget to shred all versions of your proposal that you don't need, and archive the ones you do. Create a central place in your office or on a network to store final proposals for in-house use or reference.

Delete version of graphics that aren't necessary and archive necessary versions of graphics in a place that is accessed easily by your graphic artists. This may include putting a slug number on each graphic for easy reference.

Clean up your WinCenter™/SharePoint/Privia/ Windows directory proposal repository, and delete any old versions of files.

Finally, clean up the war room so it's ready for the next proposal.

2. Lessons learned

Just as you conduct a lessons-learned analysis for the proposal preparation, you should review the production process. This can be a component of the overall lessons-learned analysis or a separate exercise. Make sure you ask your desktop publisher, editor, graphic artists, and printer how things went. Update your company production plan with the results.

Confessions of a proposal production expert—Part 1: Desktop publishing

Briana Coleman

In the previous sets of articles, I explained the production best practices all companies should perform during each phase of the BD life cycle.

In this series, I'll dive deeper into production elements and share war stories and my favorite tips. These production elements include:

- Desktop publishing
- Graphic design
- Editing
- Printing and assembly
- Delivery

Let's begin with desktop publishing, the art of formatting a document to help communicate a message and for ease of reading.

Tip 1: Start early

Desktop publishing is not a race at the end. Think about the risks for page limits! As a desktop publisher, I've received documents 24 hours before they were due, with the instructions to "work my magic and cut five pages..." Don't put that kind of pressure on your desktop publisher. Instead, begin desktop publishing and editing before Red Team so you know where you stand in terms of page count and have time to adjust.

Tip 2: Section shells

If you can't afford to have someone there 8 hours per day desktop publishing, give the writers section shells and give them an overview of how to use the templates and shells at kick-off. At least you will ensure that everyone is using the proper font/size, so their assessments of page limitations will be close.

Tip 3: Auto-generated tables of contents and acronym glossaries

Most of the software we use for desktop publishing—Microsoft (MS) Word, Adobe InDesign, etc.—are capable of automatically generating tables of contents. I can't tell you how many companies I see still manually developing them.

Insights

Capture & Proposal Insights and Tips – Volume 2

Ensure that the desktop publisher you use knows how to use these functions and also teaches them to you! The same goes for acronym glossaries — there are great software packages — many free — that will auto-develop acronym glossaries for your proposals. My favorite is AcroWizard from AnvilLogic. *(Editor's note: check out Acronyms Master Pro as well.)*

Tip 4: Remember your tabs

If you plan to have a tab between sections, or sections have specific page counts, instruct your desktop publisher to place hard breaks between sections. Don't allow sections to stop and start on the same page or your tabs won't work.

Tip 5: Electronic delivery in MS Word

The government often requires electronic copies — email or CD — to be formatted in MS Word/MS Office. This can be a nightmare. Ensure your desktop publisher understands this requirement, so they can format accordingly. A couple of tips that I've seen used include:

- When the requirement is to submit MS Word 2003 documents, don't just save down to .doc at the end. Develop in the format you are delivering (because not everything converts precisely the same from a newer version of MS Word!). Example: columns can shrink in conversion—which affects every page.

- In MS Word 2003, don't use automatic colors; they will change from document to document (this was fixed in MS Word 2007 and later versions).

- Use uniquely named style names for the same reason.

- If you open up something in one version of MS Word and it's corrupted, try using a different version of MS Word.

- Check out AppMaven's (Beth Wingate) MS Word tips and tricks for non-desktop publishers presentation handouts

  - **AppMaven's MS Word Tips & Tricks for Non-desktop Publishers 2014 cheat sheet** (http://goo.gl/r3Tal0)

  - **AppMaven MS Word Placemat** (http://goo.gl/8YEuBL)

Confessions of a proposal production expert—Part 2: Graphic design

Briana Coleman

These are my top 4 tips for developing graphics for a proposal.

Tip 1: Develop graphics as the exact size you need

For example, if the final graphic must be 3"x4" to fit on the page, have your graphic artist render the graphic at that size. Do not render the graphic at 6"x8" and then size it down when you insert it into your document. When you re-size the graphic in your document, everything gets smaller—including the fonts. If your graphic designer used a compliant font size in the initial rendering, and you size the graphic down to fit on your page, you are now non-compliant.

Story: On a large proposal, I assumed my graphic artist knew this tip. We went through a conceptualization phase, got approval at Red Team, and sent him off to render a few dozen graphics. He delivered the final graphics to me in time for Gold Team...except they were all developed at 500% the size they would be in the document. I had to have him completely redo *every* graphic in 2 days—2 days lost in our development schedule.

Tip 2: Converting graphics

Some proposal graphics are large and complex, requiring Adobe Illustrator or similar software to render. However, other graphics are relatively simple, such as organization charts and flow charts. Some graphics change dozens of times before final production. For graphics that will have numerous text changes but relatively few graphical changes (such as org charts), have your graphic artist render the imagery in his/her favorite software. Then, have them drop that imagery into a MS PowerPoint file and overlay the text and editable text boxes. This allows your authors to change the text without affecting the graphic and saves your graphic artists and writers many hours of back and forth revisions. I use this trick for my covers/spines, title pages, org charts, and other similar figures.

Insights
Capture & Proposal Insights and Tips – Volume 2

Tip 3: File format for graphics

What file format should your graphic artist use for exporting figures—.tiff, .jpg, .png, .gif? We used to say use .tiff files because this format prints the best quality graphics. However, the file size is really large.

For proposals, stick to either .jpg or .png files. Specifically, 150dpi .png files are small files with the best quality. However, .png files don't always print on printers (they have alpha channels, which gives the graphic the ability to be transparent; sometimes, printers can't handle it or it confuses the printer). So it's very important to practice printing .png files on the *actual* printer you plan to use for production if you are going to use .png graphics! Or, you can use .jpg files (most sturdy and safe for printing), and for the average evaluator, the quality is more than adequate.

Story: I used .png files for all of my graphics in a proposal. I printed all of my review team documents on an in-house printer, and the document looked fine. For the final print, we outsourced the printing to a subcontractor who had a very large production facility—we never practiced printing with them until we were printing the actual document the day before it was due. Their printers were unable to handle .png files. Everywhere I had a .png file, a blank black box printed instead. I ended up having to reformat every single page with a .jpg graphic, re-print, and re-assemble every book…all with only a few hours before the last FedEx truck left for the day.

Tip 4: MS PowerPoint graphics

If you have ever tried to copy and paste an MS PowerPoint graphic into an MS Word document, you know that something gets lost in translation. The graphics typically come in slightly fuzzy. This tends to happen even if you export the graphic as a .jpg or .png file instead of copying/pasting. My favorite MS PowerPoint add-in is PPTools Image Exporter. For a small price, this add-in exports high-resolution graphics with no more fuzziness!

Confessions of a proposal production expert—Part 3: Editing

Briana Coleman

In this article, I share my top 3 tips for editing a proposal to get within page count—along with a tip about redacted proposals.

Your editor should understand the standard style guide you developed as a company standard and use that style guide in editing your proposal. In addition to examining grammar, one-voicing, and style, editors can be very useful in helping authors tighten up sentences and get sections within page count. I once cut *five* pages from a document simply by using the following tricks.

Tip 1: Lengthy team names

Many primes with multiple subs will dub themselves *The XYZ Company Team* in proposals. While having a team name creates brand identity, it can take up a lot of room when repeated 100+ times in a document. Try using *Team XYZ*, or even better, *we/us/our* to shorten the character length considerably. You'll want to use *Team XYZ* a few times in each section to remind the reader who you are talking about, but after that, a simple *we* will suffice.

Consider the *Lohfeld Team* versus *we*…16 characters versus 2. Strive for an 80:20 ratio (80% pronouns, 20% actual company/team name).

Tip 2: Eliminate widows and orphans

Maximize each line of text, and don't leave paragraphs with one or two words dangling at the end. Every line you can eliminate adds up to pages of text saved. Eliminate lines by cutting a few words in a paragraph that aren't necessary—long adjectives and passive voice are good places to start.

Tip 3: Spacing between sentences

Most of us were taught in grammar school that the proper way to type is with two spaces between sentences. I'm here to tell you, this is **wrong**. We typed two spaces between sentences when we used typewriters. Because all letters on a typewriter are the same width, we had to use two spaces between sentences to give enough visual break. But, the invention of word processing software, like MS Word, has fixed this problem for us. MS Word automatically places the proper spacing between sentences when we type a period and a single space. By typing two spaces, not only are we adding more space than the naked eye requires to distinguish between sentences, but we are also adding to our page count! Eradicate the problem in your final document with a simple *Find and Replace*.

Tip 4: Redacted proposals

This is a trend, especially with Department of Defense (DOD) and Department of Labor (DOL) proposals. These agencies require that no company-identifying information is included in the proposal, except for a single *original* copy.

In these instances, my advice is to write the entire proposal as though it were redacted (never say your company's name). Then, as a last step, add your company information back into the document for the *original* copy only. When you write this way, you'll 1) reduce the risk of accidentally forgetting to remove your name, and 2) ensure that sentences still make sense.

On the first redacted proposal I wrote, I didn't follow this advice. We spent **hours** examining the document at the end to ensure we had taken out every instance of our name and discovered that many sentences no longer made sense. For example, we had one sentence that said, "[Redacted] reports to [Redacted], who is an employee of [Redacted]." Had we written it from the redacted point of view first, it would have read, "The Team Lead reports to the Program Manager, who is an employee of the prime contractor."

Confessions of a proposal production expert—Part 4: Printing and assembly

Briana Coleman

In theory, printing/assembling your final proposal books doesn't sound too hard. You hit *print*, wait for the printer to spit out a few thousand pages, put them in a binder, and seal the box. In reality, printing/assembly is a 1–3 day process that involves dozens of small, but important, decisions and nuances.

Tip 1: Choosing a printing company

Let's start first with the printer you use: inside equipment versus outside vendor. Be honest with yourself. Do you really have the internal skills, machines, and supplies to fully support your production?

An average office inkjet printer is not going to give you the quality or professionalism of a professional printer. It will also take *much* longer to produce your proposal. When you decide to print in-house, it is often because you've never truly done a cost/benefit analysis of outside printers. Think about the hourly rate of your employees and consultants...remember to commoditize your salaried employees (is there some better use of their time?) and compare it against the quote a printer gives to you for full production/assembly.

If you do decide to print in-house, ensure that your capabilities include contingency plans. Are you relying on a single printer? Are all of your printers in the same building on the same electrical system (what if lightening hits)? Do you have a full stock of all binder sizes and tabs? If internal printing is your preference, still consider establishing a relationship with an outside printer who can take over if something catastrophic happens.

Story from a friend (professional printer): He was scheduled to print 30 books on a Saturday afternoon. The proposal manager told him there would be 800 pages and 10 tabs per book, so they developed all of the spines and covers to fit 2" binders. What the proposal manager failed to account for were the appendices—the books skyrocketed to 1,600 pages and 20 tabs, needing 5"

binders! Luckily, the printer had a ready supply of
5" binders, as well as sophisticated capabilities to
re-size the spines and covers without having to
call the graphic artist—who was not likely to
answer her phone at 12:00 a.m. on a Saturday!

Tip 2: Practice, practice, practice (and then document your results)

Before doing your final production, practice
production activities (Red and Gold Teams are a
great opportunity to do so). What are your
metrics? How long does it really take to print on
your printer? What turnaround time does your
outside printer require? What paper type looks
best in your machine?

Also remember to test for color. What looks good
on your screen may not look the same when you
print it. If you do electronic and hard copy
proposals, find a happy medium. Generating a
.pdf is the best way to see if color or print will be
correct. Check your print settings, and you can
adjust your .pdf color-matching settings. Also,
many printers know how to adjust them
accordingly.

Story from a friend: Her office manager had
ordered a different type of paper from what they
usually got because it was less expensive. When it

went through the printer and was stacked in the volumes (about 3″–4″ thick), the reams looked purple—not an acceptable color for her military client (even with the lame argument that purple is the Joint color).

Tip 3: Know when to let go

There is a law of diminishing returns. At some point, every tweak you make to the proposal content will eat into your ability to print and assemble the documents on time. Each of those last-minute tweaks only introduces the potential for errors, without increasing your chances of winning. Do you think an evaluator is really more likely to buy because you said *happy* instead of *glad*?

Tip 4: Don't forget the details

What box are you using? Did you type up your box labels for all six sides? What packing material are you using? We are a *physical* world and a *visual* world—what are we communicating to our client from the moment they receive the box to closing the book?

Recommended standards: Use 28lb opaque paper (thick enough for print and graphics not to bleed through to the back of a page, but it still gives sharp color). For binders, use Avery Extra heavy-duty binders—they will not fall apart in mailing as cheaper binders will. For binders >4", use binder straps to ensure they don't get damaged in shipping.

Tip 5: Assume everything that can go wrong will go wrong

Fires, floods, and bomb scares have interrupted printing operations—in addition to running out of toner, not cleaning the printer before printing, not having backup machines, and the stories go on and on.

Tip 6: Print a complete back-up set

In the best-case scenario, a back-up set will serve as your in-house copy. In the worst case, it will support your contingency plan.

Tip 7: Production checklist

Before you begin desktop publishing for the first time, develop a comprehensive production checklist. This checklist will serve to guide your desktop publisher on your vision of the final product, as well as guide you on production day to ensure you've done everything you need to do. The production checklist is like a compliance matrix for your production day—it's easy to forget in the moment that the CEO must sign the SF1449 (Solicitation/Contract/Order for Commercial Items) or that the labels on the box must show the solicitation number.

Using a comprehensive checklist—customized for every job—ensures you'll meet all requirements. I typically begin forming my checklist on day 1. As I read the RFP, I keep a running document of any requirement I come across that would affect production.

A later article will include a detailed production checklist for every possible item you would have to do for a proposal—you can use it as a starting point for your next proposal.

Tip 8: Print/assembly instructions

Whether you are printing in-house or outsourcing, you want to ensure that the printer fully understands your vision for the end product. Be specific about how you want the document printed and assembled. I include a sample instruction template in a subsequent article.

Confessions of a proposal production expert—Part 5: Delivery

Briana Coleman

All great proposal teams know the few golden rules of proposal development:

- Writers are more productive when fed.

- Whatever can go wrong, will go wrong.

- You can't win if you don't deliver on time!

Here are 3 proposal delivery tips.

Tip 1: Plan on delivering EARLY

Lohfeld Consulting Group's CEO and founder Bob Lohfeld once told me this story of his early days in the proposal business. The goal was to deliver a proposal from San Diego to Pasadena. Everything that could have gone wrong did go wrong—including not budgeting enough time to print. There was not enough time to drive the proposal to the destination, so the company chartered a private helicopter on the day the proposal was due to take the 2-hour flight.

As the helicopter approached the Pasadena area, the pilot turned around and asked, "So, where do you want me to land?" When Bob told him, "The airport," the pilot laughed and informed him that you can't just get clearance to land at an airport, and they had no chance of landing anywhere near our destination.

With no choice left, they pushed the box of proposals off the helicopter at 300 feet above the ground. A few seconds later, they heard a large boom as the box—and the proposals within it—disintegrated upon impact. Their beautiful proposal was in millions of pieces, floating along the Pasadena tarmac. Needless to say, that proposal did not get delivered.

Tip 2: Always have a contingency plan

During a legendary Washington, DC summer storm, all air traffic shut down for a couple of days. Lohfeld Consulting Group's Beth Wingate had a proposal on a FedEx plane grounded at Dulles with no chance of making it to Kansas City in time. She called a local Kinkos (the closest one to the delivery site) and spent all day on the phone with the Kinkos rep in Kansas City to walk him through the entire production over the phone—binding, delivery in his personal car, faxing her the receipt from the customer, etc. She was the only person who delivered on time.

Tip 3: Stay flexible

Fellow Lohfeld Consultant Brooke Crouter had a proposal due on September 12, 2001 on the Marine Corps base at Quantico. The base shut down at about 0930 on September 11. She had to have the duty officer contact the Contracting Officer (CO) to see if the proposal delivery deadline was extended or not. Since the CO didn't want to extend, there was an issue of how to deliver to a base that was shut down. The CO was not too helpful, so Brooke suggested an e-mail delivery of the technical volume with the cost summary of the cost volume (no cost build-up in case the email went astray). Hard copies of the full submission would be delivered at a later date. Weeks went by while Brooke waited to hear about delivery. Finally, she got a call to show up NLT 1300 at the Burger King outside the back gate. There was a government vehicle parked with the trunk open. You handed off your box and got a receipt. It looked like a very strange drug deal going on.

The moral of this story is to *stay flexible* and be ready to provide a suggestion—not all COs are very experienced or creative.

Bottom Line: delivery is the most important step in the proposal process; don't do anything to risk its success!

Proposal production checklists

Lohfeld Consulting Group Team

As a follow up to Briana Coleman's proposal production series, we're sharing some helpful checklists and tools for you to use in planning your next proposal production plan.

Download the checklists and modify them to suit your company and proposals.

Proposal Production Checklist

Before you begin desktop publishing for the first time, develop a comprehensive production checklist. This checklist will serve to guide your desktop publisher on your vision of the final product, as well as guide you on production day to ensure you've done everything you need to do.

The production checklist is like a compliance matrix for your production day—it's easy to forget in the moment that the CEO must sign the SF1449, or that the labels on the box must show the solicitation number. Using a comprehensive checklist, customized for every job, ensures you'll meet all requirements. I typically begin forming my checklist on day 1. As I read the RFP, I keep a running document of any requirement I come across that would affect production.

Download **Lohfeld Consulting Group's Proposal Production Checklist** (http://goo.gl/oXAV2h).

Printing/Assembly Instructions

Whether you are printing in-house or outsourcing, you want to ensure that the printer fully understands your vision for the end product. Be specific about how you want the document printed and assembled.

Download **Lohfeld Consulting Group's Sample Printing Instructions** (http://goo.gl/ZA6aD5).

Production Resources Checklist

When planning for your proposal's production needs, use our *Production Resources Checklist* to confirm that you have all of the necessary resources to complete the production. These resources include staff, IT/facilities, network capabilities, and other necessities.

Download **Lohfeld Consulting Group's Production Resources Checklist** (http://goo.gl/lTG6BA).

Insights
Capture & Proposal Insights and Tips – Volume 2

Editing Checklist

A supplement to your company's style guide, this tool is useful for your editor to ensure that all elements of the proposal meet specific quality standards...literally, to check that all of your *i's* are dotted and *t's* are crossed. Download **Lohfeld Consulting Group's Editing Checklist** (http://goo.gl/h5JRp1).

Proposal scheduling – make it or break it— Part 1

Brenda Crist

One of the most daunting proposal management tasks is ensuring all proposal tasks are performed on schedule. The inability to meet milestones can have a ripple effect throughout the proposal and affect staff members' stress levels, proposal quality, and on-time delivery.

Scheduling best practices before, during, and after RFP release can help alleviate these risks and improve a company's chance of developing a compliant, compelling, and winning proposal.

Take time to prepare and develop an accurate schedule based on a solid understanding of required tasks and how long it took to perform them in the past. Review your company's scheduling metrics so you can accurately identify how long it takes to perform basic proposal tasks. If you don't collect metrics, consider using the

Insights

Capture & Proposal Insights and Tips – Volume 2

following chart to jump start your metrics-collection process.

Standard proposal task timeframes

Task name	Industry average	Complete for your company
Plan the proposal	10% of proposal devt. time	
Hold Daily Standup Meeting	15-30 minutes daily	
Conduct Kick-off Meeting	2-3 hours	
Conceptualize solution	1/6 of total proposal devt. time	
Produce first draft	1/3 of total proposal devt. time	
Write a page of new text	2 hours	
Revise a page of existing text	1 hour or less	
Create a new proposal cover	8-16 hours	
Create spines, CD covers, tabs	4 hours	
Create a new resume (2 pages)	4 hours	
Research and create a new past performance reference	4-8 hours	

Insights

Capture & Proposal Insights and Tips – Volume 2

Task name	Industry average	Complete for your company
Conceptualize a graphic	1-3 hours	
Render a simple graphic	1-4 hours	
Render a complex graphic	8-16 hours	
Develop final draft	2/3 of total proposal devt. time	
Review new text	40 pages daily	
Review existing text	80 pages daily	
Perform desktop publishing (DTP)	30-60 pages daily	
Produce a proposal (including DTP and production)	10% of proposal devt. time	

Next, ensure the information you need to develop the schedule is centrally located. The time allocated to planning the schedule after RFP release is never enough, so having all the information you need at your fingertips will increase scheduling speed and accuracy.

Proposal scheduling – make it or break it— Part 2

Brenda Crist

Scheduling best practices before, during, and after RFP release can help alleviate risks and improve a company's chance of developing a compliant, compelling, and winning proposal.

As soon as the RFP is released, the race against the clock starts to prepare the information needed for the Kick-off Meeting, including the schedule, compliance matrix, and writers' packages.

Start by building a bulletproof compliance matrix. Have at least two people review the compliance matrix to verify no instruction, evaluation criteria, or requirement is missed! Use the requirements list to build a work breakdown structure (WBS). Then add additional structure to incorporate proposal management tasks including:

- Kick-off Meeting
- Contributor training

- Question development
- Daily Standup Meetings conducted
- Executive Summary draft development
- Conceptual planning/solution development
- Conceptual solution review
- Conceptual solution frozen
- Non-disclosure Agreement (NDA) completion
- Teaming Agreement (TA) completion
- Reps and Certs development
- Pricing development
- Graphics conceptualization
- Document style conceptualization
- Cover, spine, and tab design
- Graphics design and development
- Price-to-win development
- Price-to-win reviews
- Risk identification
- Risk mitigation
- First draft review

- Final draft review
- Business case review
- Quality control
- Past performance qualification
- Past performance questionnaire dissemination
- Editing and quality control
- Production
- Shipping
- Delivery

Use an automated project management tool or spreadsheet to build your schedule, and apply the following "golden rules" to schedule each activity.

- Identify activities that you do not know how long it will take to perform. I call these the *long poles in the tent* and develop primary and contingent plans and schedules for performing the activities.

- Communicate the risk of unknown tasks and potential mitigation strategies to executives for approval.

- Identify which tasks can be done in parallel and which tasks must be performed sequentially.

- Schedule the last activity (delivery) first and work backwards, and provide start and stop dates for each task.

- Allow sufficient time for final desktop publishing, quality control, shipping, and delivery. The industry average is 10% of the total proposal life cycle for these tasks.

- Assign specific start and end dates to all task activities.

- Assign an individual to perform each task and ensure the individual is not overcommitted.

- Establish interim milestone reviews for the conceptual solution review, first draft review, final draft review, and business case review. Schedule interim reviews at each time 20-25% of the proposal life cycle is completed.

- Never schedule work on weekends or holidays—work not finished during the week slides into these days.

Insights
Capture & Proposal Insights and Tips – Volume 2

- Build a primary and contingent production and delivery schedule.

If you think you will miss a deadline or milestone, proactively communicate the risk to the lead executive along with your recovery plan. Estimate the time it will take to recover and what resources you need to mitigate the risk. As you implement the schedule, record the actual time taken to perform the task, compare it to your budgeted time, and provide a brief explanation as to why you missed a deadline.

After proposal submission

After submitting the proposal, update your scheduling metrics illustrated in part 1 of this post, and store the proposal documents in a central, secure location. Extract relevant information for your library of boilerplate text, and update your past performance and resume databases.

Try to schedule a *lessons-learned* session within one week of proposal submission to identify what you did right and make recommendations for improvements in scheduling and schedule management for your next proposal.

As soon as you get an award notification from the Contracting Officer (CO), schedule a debrief session (whether you won or lost), and store the debrief notes in your central repository.

Requirements matrices, compliance matrices, and why you need both

Brenda Crist

A proposal manager's biggest concern is working on a huge proposal for months and having it rejected because an instruction was not followed or an esoteric requirement was not addressed.

Adding to this risk are disconnects among the statement of work, proposal instructions, and evaluation criteria.

To avoid compliance issues, consider building a requirements matrix and a compliance matrix. The requirements matrix assigns to each requirement a specific number and verifies that it is met in the proposal, as Figure 1 illustrates. To facilitate internal proposal development add columns including the page size limit and author name to the matrix.

Figure 1. Requirements matrix

Rqt #	Sol §#	Sol § Name	Sol Pg #	Rqt	Rqt Met (Yes/No)	Comments
1	1	Personnel	1	N/A	Yes	None
2	1.1	Organization	1	Prepare org. chart	Yes	None
3	1.2	Roles and Responsibilities	3	Define roles and responsibilities of key personnel	Yes	None
4	1.3	Key Personnel Resumes	9	Provide resumes for all key personnel	No	No program manager resume

Use the requirements matrix to build a compliance matrix. The compliance matrix simply cross walks each requirement to a proposal section number and name. Depending on the complexity and synchronization of the requirements, you can order the compliance matrix by solicitation section number and name, as illustrated in Figure 2, or by the proposal section number and name. Submit the compliance matrix with the proposal to facilitate its evaluation by your customer.

Insights

Capture & Proposal Insights and Tips – Volume 2

Figure 1. Compliance matrix

Sol §#	Sol § Name	Prop §#	Prop § Name	Prop Pg #
1	Personnel	1	Personnel	1
1.1	Organization	1.1	Organization chart	1
1.2	Roles and Responsibilities	1.2	Description of Key Personnel Roles and Responsibilities	2
1.3	Key personnel resumes	1.3	Key personnel resumes	5

Allow ample time for preparing the matrices—a solicitation with hundreds of requirements could take 2 or 3 days to prepare and verify. Assign one or more people to review the requirements and compliance matrices before the Kick-off Meeting. Assign compliance checkers during the reviews of the initial and final proposal drafts to validate compliance.

Use the requirements and compliance matrices to build the proposal schedule, create proposal writers' packages, and estimate the number of reviewers needed. The time taken to prepare accurate and well-documented matrices saves times on re-writes, reduces the risk of non-compliance, facilities evaluation, and maximizes your proposal score.

Recompetes

Insights

Capture & Proposal Insights and Tips – Volume 2

Working with project managers on recompetes—Part 1: Risk aversion versus price

Lisa Pafe

Incumbents often proceed with the recompete capture and proposal process with only peripheral involvement from the project manager. I believe that this attitude is part of the general problem of *incumbentitis*—the false sense of security, complacency, and over-confidence that results in failing to take the capture/proposal process seriously and thus losing the recompete bid. In fact, recent industry statistics indicate that incumbents lose approximately 50% of their recompetes.

In the current climate of budget constraints, the customer experiences even greater tension between their natural risk aversion and the real or perceived need for fresh perspectives. They must balance low risk versus low price. Only by working closely with the project manager in the capture stage can the capture manager gain an honest assessment of the customer relationship in order to reinforce the customer's risk aversion. Working with the project manager, the capture manager and executive leadership should focus on the following questions:

- Are there any problems or performance issues that have arisen?

- Have you addressed these issues successfully?

- Have you taken proactive, preventive measures to prevent recurrence of any problems or to introduce cost savings, innovations, and/or best practices?

Any performance issues will reduce the advantage the incumbent has of being low risk. Capture and project management must work hand-in-hand during project execution to build the customer relationship and ensure the past performance ((Past Performance Information Retrieval System (PPIRS), Contractor Performance Assessment Reporting System (CPARS)) reflects high-quality work and customer satisfaction.

Insights
Capture & Proposal Insights and Tips – Volume 2

Price is another potential issue for incumbents. The current environment favors LPTA. In a re-compete, it is difficult for the incumbent to come in as lowest bidder due to more senior labor categories. Therefore, start early to transition more junior staff onto the project (staff remaining from contract start may be overqualified and command a higher salary than more entry-level—yet qualified—replacements). Additionally, work with the project manager to look for areas where technology and process improvement can increase cost competitiveness.

Price and risk are a balancing act for the incumbent. Only by partnering with the project manager can capture managers and executive leadership find the right mix that speaks to the customer's needs.

Working with project managers on recompetes—Part 2: Project manager as an ethical spy

Lisa Pafe

Project managers have an enormous role to play in gathering competitive intelligence that the capture manager can use to build recompete win strategies.

Because the project manager is on-site, the capture manager can coach the project manager to serve as an *ethical spy* in preparing for a recompete:

- Who is visiting with the customer?
- Who has offered brown bags, seminars, and other freebies?
- What other companies are working for this customer?

Because the project manager knows the scope of work intimately, (s)he knows what is most

Insights

Capture & Proposal Insights and Tips – Volume 2

important to the customer. Capture and project management working together can ethically influence the new solicitation to favor incumbent discriminators. For example, if evaluation factors rate key personnel, relevant past performance, and seamless transition as of greatest importance, then the incumbent has an edge. Similarly, if the pendulum can swing from LPTA to best value, the incumbent team has a greater advantage.

It much easier for the project manager to get to know potential Source Selection Board (SSB) members than it is for the capture manager. The project manager can find out who will be on the SSB, who the key decision-makers are, and who makes the final decision. This information feeds into building hot buttons and discriminators.

Finally, there is the issue of teaming. In recompete situations, there are two possible scenarios: you remain the prime or you become a subcontractor. If you plan to prime the recompete, then capture and project management must work together to:

- Keep your performing teaming partners loyal
- Replace non-performers early

- Possibly eliminate a potential competitor by adding them to the team

- Determine who the customer likes—these may be potential teammates

If you need to become a subcontractor on the recompete, either because you have outgrown a size standard or the work is moving from large to small business, then the capture manager and project manager need to strategize:

- Can one of your teammates be the prime?

- If not, who else fits?

- Can potential teaming partners be brought in now as subcontractors to fill open positions so the client gets to know them?

All of these aspects of competitive intelligence require a strong partnership between capture and project management professionals.

Insights

Working with project managers on recompetes—Part 3: Project manager as proposal SME

Lisa Pafe

In addition to providing customer and competitive intelligence, the project manager also has a role to play in helping the proposal manager gather artifacts that can be used as proof points for discriminators. Additionally, the project manager serves as an essential subject matter expert for the recompete.

Before RFP release, the proposal manager should make a list of the artifacts the project team must gather to help support and prove the win themes, features and benefits, and discriminators. Some items the project manager can continuously gather and share include:

- Congratulatory emails
- Awards and certificates of appreciation

- Customer quotes and kudos

- Award fees achieved

- Achievements (e.g., performed testing with zero rollbacks, brought in web redesign under budget, identified efficiencies and/or new technology that saved the customer money)

- Project library (examples of strategic plans, deliverables, research)

The project manager supports the ongoing task of keeping the project's past performance write-up current. As part of this effort, the proposal manager should ensure that the project manager prepares the customer so they are ready to provide a glowing reference. Additionally, the project manager should work with project personnel and the company's Human Resources department in updating project staff resumes every 6 months.

Once the RFP is released, the project manager serves as a resource to help with management, transition, technical approach, and past performance sections of the proposal. The project manager should compare the new solicitation to the existing scope of work to understand the significance of any changes and communicate them to the proposal team as a whole:

- Do changes reflect changes/technological advances in your industry?

- Does the new RFP reflect the processes and methodologies you already employ?

- Does the RFP require certifications you do or do not have?

- Does the scope of work indicate the customer's desire to increase or decrease the current level of service?

- Do any requirements in the RFP seem to relate directly to incumbent performance issues?

Expectations are high for the incumbent's proposal. Accordingly, the project manager must participate actively during the proposal stage to help develop a winning bid.

Insights

Capture & Proposal Insights and Tips – Volume 2

Data Calls

The art of the data call: 7 questions to ask pre-RFP

Lisa Pafe

I have served as a Color Team Reviewer on many proposals that, while compliant, had a glaring lack of proof points. When I debriefed the team, I told them that they had forgotten an important proposal task—the team-wide data call.

Unfortunately, too many companies limit data calls to resumes, past performance, and a company bio of revenues and full time employees (FTE). But, a data call should go beyond compliance; it must form the basis of persuasion.

Persuasion is what makes your proposal compelling. Data calls provide the grist for win themes, discriminators, features and benefits, call-out boxes, and action captions. At the most basic level, the data call is an information-gathering request, internal to your company and external to teaming partners, which specifies:

- Who: the point of contact (POC) for the data call

- What: the data you need

- When: the deadline for each data call (pre- and post-RFP)

- How: detailed instructions with clear due dates

Often, we delegate the data call to more junior staff, when in reality, an artful data call is tied very explicitly to the capture strategy. The proposal manager and capture manager should work together *before the RFP is released* to craft the data call by asking 7 questions:

1. What information do we need to prove discriminators and win themes?

2. Which data best illustrates our features and benefits?

3. What proof points do we need?

4. How can we discriminate our bid from the competition?

5. What do the teaming partners bring to the table?

6. What worked and what didn't in past proposals?

7. What information does this customer typically require in their solicitations?

Pre-RFP release, issue the data call and begin to aggregate and assess the data. After RFP release, you can issue a second data call for compliance purposes or to provide additional RFP-specific information.

By starting early, you gain the advantage of time. Often, gathering effective data is impossible when faced with a 10-day or even 30-day turnaround time. This approach puts you well on your way to a compelling proposal during the capture stage.

The art of the data call: proof points that POP

Lisa Pafe

I already discussed *7 questions to form the basis of the data call*. But, how do you ensure that your proof points are any good? Here are some examples of typical bland proposal statements that beg the reader to ask for proof:

- We enjoy high levels of customer satisfaction. *How high?*

- We have low employee turnover. *Compared to what?*

- We offer relevant experience. *In what?*

- We have the personnel reach back to rapidly staff task orders. *Prove it!*

By crafting an effective data call, you get proof points that **POP** as shown in the following examples.

Insights
Capture & Proposal Insights and Tips – Volume 2

P: Persuasive

We will meet or exceed performance expectations. In all 12 of our Past Performance Information Retrieval System (PPIRS) ratings for eight agencies over the past 3 years, we achieved no lower than *Excellent* or *Outstanding* ratings. On all six of our performance-based contracts, we have achieved maximum award fees and incentives.

O: (Focused on customer) Objectives

We know staff retention is of utmost importance to the project. Our retention rate across the company is 90%, compared to 82% industry-wide for similar IT positions. On help desk projects such as this one, our retention rate is 98% due to our focus on leveraging Help Desk Institute certifications and best practice processes.

P: (Verifiable) Proofs

Our company has performed 24 software development projects for 13 customers over the past 3 years, all of which were performed at CMMI Level 3 or higher. We have the reach back to staff the task orders through 5,700 qualified and cleared IT personnel across the team, of which 750 hold the required ITIL Foundation certification, 25 are ITIL Experts, and 5,000 hold Secret clearances or above.

As these three examples illustrate, you can attain proof points that POP with:

- Specific examples and lessons learned that provide evidence

- Verifiable facts such as PPIRS ratings that can be confirmed by the SSB

- External, unbiased third parties such as industry appraisals or customer quotes that offer confirmation

- Data aggregation that shows size and strength

- Comparisons that ghost competition.

Gathering the information in advance gives your team a significant competitive advantage by going beyond compliance to a compelling bid.

Insights

Capture & Proposal Insights and Tips – Volume 2

The art of the data call: 4 data calls you can issue today

Lisa Pafe

The previous two articles discussed what you can do pre-RFP to tie your data call to the win strategy and how to get proof points that POP (Persuasive, Objectives, Proofs). However, what are the elements of the data call, and who should complete it? Below are specific examples of data elements that will help you create and issue data calls during the capture stage.

Staffing data call

- POCs: HR and Recruiting
- Personnel details (clearances, education, certifications, domain areas)
- Recruiting statistics (average time to fill positions, number of recruiters, size of recruiting database, recruiting sources)
- Retention rate (company-wide and project-specific)

- Meatball charts (experience versus functional or technical requirements)
- Representative resumes

Past performance data call

- POCs: Project managers, SMEs, Proposals, and Contracts
- Customer information
- Project information (period of performance, size in FTEs/$$/users, scope, complexity, relevancy)
- Award fees and incentives earned
- PPIRS and CPARS ratings
- Achievements and innovations (performed testing with zero rollbacks; brought in web redesign under budget; identified efficiencies and/or new technology that saved the customer money)
- Meatball charts (past performance examples versus functional or technical requirements)

Insights
Capture & Proposal Insights and Tips – Volume 2

Corporate experience data call

- POCs: Contracts, Office of the Chief Financial Officer (OCFO,) Marketing, Proposals, SMEs
- Logos
- Corporate history
- Corporate revenues, personnel, customers, and locations
- Dun & Bradstreet (D&B) ratings
- Certifications and appraisals
- Industry awards and rankings
- R&D efforts
- Centers of Excellence
- Recognized experts
- Publications and white papers

Customer Kudos

- POCs: Contracts, project managers coordinate with customers for approval, if needed
- Congratulatory emails
- Awards and certificates of appreciation

- Quotes
- Success stories

Pricing/business volume data call

- POCs: Finance and Contracts
- Rates
- Other direct costs (ODC)
- Accounting system
- Uncompensated overtime policy
- Compensation plan
- Reps and certs
- Lines of credit
- Banking information

You can issue these data calls internally as well as externally to teaming partners with signed non-disclosure agreements and teaming agreements. Once the RFP is released, refine the data calls further to request information required for compliance purposes.

Since you will have gathered most of the necessary information early, writers will have the ammunition they need for a tailored response full of proof points that POP.

Insights

Capture & Proposal Insights and Tips – Volume 2

Spending

Insights

Doing more with less – and winning more!

Lohfeld Consulting Group Team

The typical company spends on average 10% of their revenue target on Bids and Proposals (B&P). Risks that increase the B&P budget include poor bid decisions, an immature solution, insufficient training and tools, large review teams producing comments that are not actionable, and lack of executive support. With constrained budgets and increased competition for a smaller work share, contractors cannot afford to waste B&P dollars.

Lohfeld Consulting Group's Principal Consultants Brenda Crist, CPP APMP Fellow, and Lisa Pafe, CPP APMP, presented an interactive webinar to 157 participants to highlight how to increase productivity and win rates.

Live audience polling showed that 37% of webinar participants always establish and enforce B&P budgets, 32% sometimes do, and 31% never do. With these statistics in mind, it is especially important to understand how to estimate the budget and how to manage it for maximum productivity, defined as a greater number of B&P activities that are of high quality to result in more wins.

Brenda and Lisa recommended borrowing from best practices such as:

- International Organization for Standardization (ISO)

- Information Technology Infrastructure Library (ITIL)

- Capture Maturity Model Integration (CMMI)

- Project Management Institute Project Management Body of Knowledge (PMI PMBOK)

- Agile

These all have in common the Plan, Do, Check, Act (PDCA) cycle. Establishing Standard Operating Procedures (SOPs) based on best practices provides a foundation in an environment of rapid change. Best practices serve as a springboard to tailor your solution to customer needs and hone your discriminators. Interestingly, audience live polling showed that 26% of companies always apply best practices to increase productivity, 68% sometimes do, and 6% never do.

Insights
Capture & Proposal Insights and Tips – Volume 2

Brenda and Lisa provided tips for pre-RFP, post-RFP, and post-submission productivity enhancements.

Pre-RFP:

- **Pipeline development** – Make informed decisions at the earliest phase to have the biggest impact on cost savings.

- **Capture management** – Avoid incomplete capture; poor capture pushes costs into the proposal phase resulting in much higher B&P costs.

- **Teaming partner identification** – Pre-qualify reliable partners – costs rise when teaming partners are in flux.

- **Competitive intelligence** – Focus competitive intelligence on Research, Analysis, and Action.

- **Database development** (Resumes/Past Performance) – Leverage existing boilerplate, resumes, company factoids, and past performance as one of the easiest ways to reduce proposal costs.

- **Training and tools** – Make a business case for training and tools to increase productivity (and try to use G&A (General and Administrative) not B&P budget).

Post-RFP:

- **Proposal management** – Use Agile, iterative cycles to provide continuous feedback and communication. Manage pricing development and review just as rigorously as the technical approach.

- **Data calls** – Create a comprehensive data call template and progress tracking sheet easily tailored to each solicitation.

- **Writing and editing** – Define the solution fully before writing; provide a detailed outline, writing template, conventions and style guide.

- **Proposal reviews** – Right size the team, issue clear instructions, score from the government evaluator perspective.

- **Production** – Implement reusable templates easily tailored; enforce scheduled time for production, quality assurance (QA), and white glove to avoid last minute errors.

Insights
Capture & Proposal Insights and Tips – Volume 2

- **Teaming partner management** – Set proposal participation expectations in teaming agreement and enforce them.

Post-submission:

- **Customer debrief** – Win or lose, make it part of the lessons learned and Continuous Process Improvement (CPI) cycle.

- **Lessons learned** – Create a feedback loop that includes root cause analysis to avoid repeating the same mistakes and expecting different results.

- **Continual process improvement** – Share more, not less; change before you have to!

The final interactive poll asked the audience which factors have the biggest impact on B&P costs and must therefore be managed to increase productivity—24% of participants selected improved opportunity reviews, 52% better capture planning, 4% streamlined proposal planning, 10% better proposal execution, and 9% CPI.

The first reaction to tough times by many companies is to make cuts. We have all seen the downsizing at various companies, often starting with business development, capture, and proposals. While understandable to bottom-line focused management, this approach will not help retain market share. Contractors must focus on increasing productivity. As webinar polling showed, opportunity qualification and better capture have the biggest impact on cost savings; poor bid decisions and incomplete capture have the potential to inflate B&P costs many times over through multiple re-writes. Best practices increase productivity, reduce errors and non-compliance, and improve competitiveness and win rates.

Insights

Capture & Proposal Insights and Tips – Volume 2

Q&A – Doing more with less – and winning more!

Brenda Crist and Lisa Pafe

The typical company spends on average 10% of their revenue target on B&P. Risks that increase the B&P budget include poor bid decisions, an immature solution, insufficient training and tools, large review teams producing comments that are not actionable, and lack of executive support. With constrained budgets and increased competition for smaller work share, contractors cannot afford to waste B&P dollars.

In their interactive webinar, *Doing more with less – and winning more,* Lisa Pafe and Brenda Crist highlighted how to increase productivity and win rates.

View the webinar replay and download the presentation (http://goo.gl/onRHHI).

Here are some questions submitted by webinar participants and the answers Lisa and Brenda provided.

Q: Budgets are established without good planning inputs—how do you address this?

A: Start comparing actuals to budgets containing poor-quality data immediately, and use the new data to adjust your budgets. Also, start identifying and baselining key performance indicators.

Q: How has the growing percentage of streamlined acquisitions with quick-turn task orders (Indefinite Delivery, Indefinite Quantity (IDIQ) vehicles) affected the B&P life cycle and best practices?

A: Whatever process your company adopts, it must be able to adapt to changes in the market. We recommend establishing a process that can easily be tailored to circumstances. For shorter turnaround procurements, try to apply the Agile methodology with iterative, rolling reviews. Leverage your templates and re-use materials for quick responses.

Insights
Capture & Proposal Insights and Tips – Volume 2

Q: What artifacts or data does the capture team use to architect a winning solution prior to a solicitation's release?

A: The most important artifact is any information provided by customer, including customer interview notes, emails, reports, etc. Also, gather secondary information about the customer including the customer's budget tolerance, acquisition history, and strategic documents. Then collect information about competitors' solutions and technical information from service or product vendors to develop the winning solution.

Q: What part do competitive analysis and Black Hats play in the capture and B&P process?

A: Competitive analysis helps identify key competitors, predict competitor strategy to better position ourselves, assess how competitors stack up against customer needs and evaluation criteria, identify gaps in our strategy, develop our teaming strategy, obtain information to help influence and shape the procurement, and develop price to win.

The role of Black Hats is to give the team insight into how a competitor might beat us and evaluate our strengths and weaknesses versus the competition. Black hat team members assume the identity of each competitor as well as our own company and present the respective competitors' win strategies to a mock evaluation board. The results give insights into how to strengthen our proposal.

Q: Is 10% the industry standard spend for B&P?

A: 1% is the industry best practice; however, I see so many B&P dollars wasted that 10% is not uncommon—especially for smaller bids

Q: Given a 1% B&P budget of the opportunity value, how would you apportion this 1% during proposal phases—capture, proposal development, and post-submission?

A: 20% prior to the proposal, 75% during the proposal, and 5% for clarifications.

Q: Will you please describe techniques or tools you have found successful to get color review teams to score rather than read?

A: We recommend developing a scoring template that can be tailored to each bid. Our best practice is to incorporate Lohfeld Consulting Group's **Seven Quality Measures** (http://goo.gl/yoPlzU) into the score sheet. Assign review team members to review and score the proposal based on specific measures. For example, one review team member might review and score for compliance and another for visual appeal. Base the scoring both on the RFP's evaluation methodology as well as on a simple four-color scale for more qualitative areas, such as visual appeal.

Q: B&P and Independent Research and Development (IR&D) share the same indirect cost account as far as the Defense Contract Audit Agency (DCAA) is concerned. How do your B&P metrics apply when trying to create budget differentiation between these two types of indirect costs?

A: Technical effort expended in developing and preparing technical data specifically to support bid or proposal activities is considered B&P, rather than IR&D. Administrative costs related to B&P activities are also covered under the B&P definition. B&P does not include the costs of efforts sponsored by a grant or cooperative agreement or required in the performance of a contract.

Q: Do you have any suggestions for where to obtain a good example for conducting a proposal debrief or an internal lessons learned?

A: Develop a simple template for internal lessons learned based on people, processes, and technology/tools. How did the team perform (writers, reviewers, etc.), and who needs additional training? Did our processes work well, or do we need to change them? Did our tools and templates as well as our technology (collaborative software, on-line meeting tools) perform to expectations?

For each area of weakness, develop a plan to get better. For each area of strength, figure out how to leverage high performers. Also, make sure to hold the lessons-learned session very soon after the proposal submission, and communicate results to all stakeholders.

Q: What are the best methods to obtain accurate competitive analysis?

A: Become a student of your marketplace and competition, and you will eventually build competitive analysis profiles.

Q: How do you know what your competitors are bidding?

A: You don't. You can only guestimate based on the best information available.

Insights

Capture & Proposal Insights and Tips – Volume 2

Q: How do government reviewers score without reading?

A: Government evaluators *score* rather than *read* because they have limited time and many proposals to review. They have to complete their score sheets, so they tend to skim through the proposal looking primarily for the information that will help them complete their score sheets. That is why it is so important to make it easy for the evaluators with crosswalks and cross-references to the evaluation factors as well as good visual appeal, leveraging tables, graphics, call-out boxes, action captions, and bullets—and avoiding dense text.

How much should we spend on capture versus proposal activities?

Lohfeld Consulting Group Team

We worked with Market Connections to conduct a short poll of federal government contractors regarding the effects of sequestration and the government shutdown on the government contracting community—and the changes these reductions required contractors to make to their businesses in 2014.

One poll participant asked us, "During your research into Capture Management best practice, for planning purposes, do you have an estimation of the average hours spent or industry standard for hours spent by a capture manager between opportunity identification to bid decision?"

In response, Bob Lohfeld provided his insights.

"I don't think anyone has quantified it in terms of hours since that would vary greatly by the size (value of the job). A better way to look at the question is to ask the shape of spending over the life cycle of acquiring business. For this, there are some guidelines.

If your spending before the RFP is released represents half of your total spend to acquire a new business opportunity, then your chance of winning will be pretty good. In contrast, if your spending before the RFP is very little, then you chance of winning drops greatly.

The challenge for capture managers and new business executives is to get out in front of deals rather than be the last contender to show up for a bid. Capture is a well-defined process that takes time and effort to execute. If you don't have the time and put in the effort, someone else will, and that greatly increases their chance of winning and reduces yours.

Strive for the 50/50 rule on major bids. Spend half the money on capture and half on the proposal. That will keep you out in front on important deals."

Health & Stress

Insights

Capture & Proposal Insights and Tips – Volume 2

6 stress busters that increase productivity

Lisa Pafe

Stress is one of the greatest productivity busters, **costing American businesses $300 billion per year in lost productivity** (http://goo.gl/YXovrK). The **World Health Organization** (http://goo.gl/uJ02eZ) states that stress creates an unhealthy organization, reducing team productivity in a competitive market and even threatening the organization's very survival.

There are times when stress is necessary, but sometimes we become overwhelmed. I have a tendency to become so engaged in managing or contributing to an important proposal or project that it overwhelms other aspects of my life. I go to bed only to see my latest writing or reviewing project swimming behind my closed eyelids. It can be hard to turn off the stress when I hear the email notification chiming on my laptop or iPhone. Great ideas seem to pop up in the middle of the night making it even harder to relax and sleep.

You do yourself and your team no favors by feeling stressed and sleep-deprived. When you are on edge, it permeates the team dynamic, making you less patient, more prone to (inadvertently) insulting others, and reducing productivity. So, how can you be actively engaged and productive without getting stressed out? Here are six methods that work for me.

1. Yoga

Yoga is a great way to reduce stress, increase flexibility, and regain composure—all highly beneficial to the harried proposal or project professional, especially during times of increased competition, fiscal constraints, and uncertainty. You don't need to roll out a yoga mat in order to relax. Just take 10 minutes at your desk and try these **proposal yoga poses and meditations** (http://goo.gl/hYEy8c). Invite your teammates to join in. Stress will decrease, and you will be ready to take on the next challenge.

2. Food

One of the ways teams reward themselves– or force everyone to stay in the same room– is with food. Consuming too much caffeine, sugar, salt, carbs, and grease makes everyone feel sluggish and testy. Make a pact with your team that you will share healthy meals and snacks. At least you won't put on the proposal or project 3 pounds around your waistline, and you demonstrate that you care about your colleagues.

3. Scents

Manage the mood through scents. Make sure no one has sensitivities, and then invest in an essential oil diffuser with calming scents such as lavender, grapefruit, or chamomile, when needed, or try invigorating scents like peppermint or lemon when the team needs a boost. If the team does not agree to this odor-based approach, use the scents at home to reduce stress or to wake up.

4. Downtime

Yes, we are under severe schedule constraints, but working non-stop becomes unproductive. Set some firm times to stop working and let people go home to relax and/or exercise. Promise no emails after a certain time of night so team members won't be watching their mailbox. Allow flexible schedules within reason so the team can find time to exercise, see their family, walk the dog, or do whatever is important to them.

5. Face Time

Related to downtime is a ban on face time. I have experienced team dynamics where team members feel compelled to stay in the room even when their tasks are completed. They don't want to go home early and risk the wrath of the manager. Tell the team that efficiency pays off. Once they are done for the day, they can leave.

6. Laughter

Teams that laugh together work well together. Laughter affects the mind and the immune system in positive ways through its stress-reducing properties. Taking your mind off work for a few minutes to share a laugh lets everyone take a break and then get back to being productive. It also bonds the team together through shared humor.

Stress is a fact of life. **We need stress** (http://goo.gl/nrmAEV) in order to perform or achieve certain goals. However, managing team stress levels effectively is key to continued peak performance.

5 proposal yoga poses to add to your life cycle

Lisa Pafe

Yoga is a great way to reduce stress, increase flexibility, and regain composure—all highly beneficial to the harried proposal professional. Here are some ways to incorporate these yoga-induced benefits into your proposal life cycle.

You don't need to roll out a yoga mat in order to relax. Just take 10 minutes at your desk and try these five proposal yoga poses. Remember to ease into these poses and stop immediately if you feel any pain or discomfort.

1. Kick-off sun salutation

Greet the day (or the sunset). Stand up beside your desk, shoes off. Slowly raise your arms above your head, breathing in through your nose until your palms touch. Then, slowly swan dive down to the floor breathing out through your nose and letting your head, neck, and arms dangle. You can shake your head *yes* and *no* to further relieve tension. If hamstrings are too tight, bend your knees slightly. Then slowly rise, breathing in, one vertebra at a time, and raise your hands until your palms touch above your head. Finally, slowly bring your palms together in front of your heart while breathing out. Repeat as many times as needed.

2. Blue Team neck stretch

Perfect when the proposal team is a pain in the neck! Continue to stand or sit back down in your chair. Slowly move your head to the left, and let your gaze follow upward, and then the right. Follow with the *Yes* pose, in which you tilt your head as far back as comfortable and then tilt forward with your chin near your chest, relaxing into the pose each time and breathing slowly. Repeat the positions two more times.

3. Pink Team wrist stretch

You've been up all night writing and reviewing, and now your wrists hurt. Sit up straight in your chair and press your hands down on the chair, fingers pointing outward. Raise your shoulders up and down slowly. Repeat several times. You can also do this pose standing by placing your hands on your desk.

4. Gold Team back twist

Relieve the pressure and tension of impending deadlines. Sit in your chair, cross one leg over the other, and grasp your top knee with your opposite hand. Hold the back of your chair with your free hand and slowly twist your upper body and head towards that arm. Hold for 10 counts. Switch your legs and arms, and twist in the opposite direction.

5. Home stretch meditation pose

Useful when you can't figure out how to cut five more pages to get within page count and still remain compliant! Sit down in your chair with your feet on the floor. Relax your hands on your lap, palms facing upward. Close your eyes and relax your face and jaw. Focus inward on your third eye (between your eyebrows). Slowly take a deep breath in through your nose for 5 counts, hold briefly, and then breath out of your mouth for 8 to 10 counts. Repeat several times.

I've been practicing yoga—both in the studio and at my desk—for several years and can attest to the mental and physical health benefits. Remember, even if you only have 10 minutes free, you can regain a little bit of sanity through these poses.

Namaste!

The Proposal Doctor

Insights
Capture & Proposal Insights and Tips – Volume 2

Ask the Proposal Doctor
Sick of debating

Dear Proposal Doctor,

Our team is in a pitched battle over the proposal outline, and until we resolve it, this proposal is going nowhere. The government's Section M evaluation criteria (different from what is in Section L) are stated in paragraph form with no numbering or lists or bullets.

The paragraphs read like a stream-of-consciousness novel with little form or organization. They are repetitive. Yet some on our team want to take each phrase and make that phrase a heading in the proposal. If we had unlimited page count, this might make sense, but we don't. Should we organize according to Section L instructions and try to weave in the key words from Section M whenever possible?

The endless debate and churn is cutting into the valuable time available to write and develop compelling graphics. How can we achieve closure? Soon!

–Sick of Debating

Insights
Capture & Proposal Insights and Tips – Volume 2

Dear Sick,

Your question is a good one, even if the topic seems theological at first glance.

In the old days, we were all taught to organize proposals first by Section L, then by Section M, then by Section C. Sometimes that works, especially when Sections L and the M are aligned. Often they are not. Often there are items in L that do not appear in M and vice versa. Content in the proposal has to be tied to Section M or it won't get evaluation points. (In contrast, the items called out only in Section L can lose it for you if they are missing, but not win it for you, no matter how great the content.)

Without seeing the RFP text, it is difficult to know the best way to handle your particular situation. You can't abandon Section M altogether and hope to win.

Here is one approach that might work. Look at each sentence in Section M and try to determine the center of gravity for that sentence. What is the main point? What does the customer really care about? Create a heading that addresses the main point of each sentence using at least some of the same words as those in Section M without necessarily repeating the entire sentence in your heading. If you come across a sentence that contains the same content as a previous sentence, use backward referencing so that you don't have to repeat content.

I have seen proposals where the Section M sentences are in text boxes next to a paragraph to remind the evaluators what is being addressed, but that does eat up page count.

I am afraid there is no easy answer, but you do have to pay close attention to what is in Section M and find a way to map it, however challenging that might be. Perhaps not what you wanted to hear!

All the Best,

Wendy Frieman, The Proposal Doctor

Ask the Proposal Doctor
Dying of boredom

Dear Proposal Doctor,

My team is dying of boredom, and I am afraid they will all quit. We haven't seen an RFP in over 3 months, and this is a hard-working proposal team that thrives on adrenaline.

How can I keep everyone motivated? These dry spells are very hard to manage.

–Dying

Dear Dying,

The proposal business is spiky and probably always will be. Periods of frantic activity followed by weeks of nothingness—this appears to be the new *normal*. Government procurements are now regularly delayed, and commercial acquisitions have their own form of quirkiness and unpredictability.

The time in between proposals is incredibly valuable. This is the time to rest up and then to sharpen the knives and get prepared for the next big surge. Here are some areas where all proposal teams can improve:

Insights

Capture & Proposal Insights and Tips – Volume 2

- Does your team really understand the products or solutions? This knowledge can be very helpful and can reduce reliance on SMEs.

- Does everyone on your team have and understand how to use the most recent versions of your desktop tools? The time in between proposals is the ideal time for training.

- What needs to be improved in your proposal process? Have you looked at every step to see how you can create efficiencies and reduce stress?

- Have you organized the material that you reuse on each proposal?

- Have you and your team read the latest books and articles on proposal development to see if there are new methodologies that you should test? Now would be a good time for a trial run.

- When you attack these tasks, remember what all parents know about small children: structure is everything. Don't tell someone to reorganize 10 years of boilerplate. Assign specific, bite-sized projects with defined end dates. Create contests, teams, presentations, or any other approach that conforms to your organization and its culture.

You will be glad you made this investment. Many people envy the opportunity you have, so please make good use of it!

All the Best,

Wendy Frieman, The Proposal Doctor

Insights
Capture & Proposal Insights and Tips – Volume 2

Ask the Proposal Doctor
Frustrated at stupidity

Dear Proposal Doctor,

The powers that be in my company took drastic measures after a number of proposals were submitted containing errors resulting from use of old proposal material. As of now, no one has access to old proposals so that everyone will have to write everything from scratch. Of course, there are still some electronic and hard copies floating around, so the hunt is on to see who has the biggest stash.

Is there an official best practice with respect to using previous proposals? If we don't get this policy reversed, it seems to me that we are going to be re-inventing the wheel at considerable cost to the company and ultimately to our customers.

–Frustrated at Stupidity

Dear Frustrated,

Good artists copy. Great artists steal. Who said that? I don't know, but I think it was Picasso or someone equally gifted.

Yes, there is a best practice, and it is all about balance. It makes no sense to start with a blank piece of paper if there are existing artifacts that are relevant, and it is dangerous to rely too heavily on previously developed content. When I have used old proposal sections (or even pages or paragraphs), I have ended up changing every single sentence. But it still saved me time to have text from which to start.

Your company's reaction reminds me of a comment a European friend made to me years ago. She said, "Americans either *overwhelm* or *underwhelm*. You would be better off if you could just *whelm*." The policy you describe is over-correction. It is easy because it is absolute, but it is also (forgive me) *dumb* for two reasons.

First, it is likely to result in a *black market,* a trend you have already alluded to in your letter. Maybe the executives in your company are familiar with what happened in the United States during Prohibition? It was not pretty, whatever one thinks of alcohol consumption. The reuse that is traded on this black market is sure to be of inferior quality and might even contain serious errors. Chasing after it will become a preoccupation with significant opportunity cost.

Second, the policy is focused on the symptom and not the disease. The issue appears to be a lack of quality control, not a reliance on re-use.

See if you can find an executive who is willing to listen to common sense and try these arguments out. Maybe one person working behind the scenes can be more effective than someone orchestrating a frontal attack, as tempting as that might be.

All the Best,

Wendy Frieman, The Proposal Doctor

Ask the Proposal Doctor

Shaking an incumbent out of its complacent rut?

Dear Proposal Doctor,

I am working with a team that is about to bid on a contract for which they are the incumbents. They have been doing this work for a while and they get plenty of kudos from the customer.

However, re-competes are always difficult. These people cannot generate any ideas about how to do things better or differently in the future. They are convinced that they have the answers and that the way they have been delivering services up until now is actually the best way. What can I do to throw a grenade into this scenario? I know that with this attitude, we will lose.

–Scared

Insights

Capture & Proposal Insights and Tips – Volume 2

Dear Scared,

You are correct. The complacency of incumbent teams is now a thing of legends, and everyone has at least one story of the incumbent we were sure the customer loved who lost and, in some instances, lost big.

The good news is that techniques exist to get your team out of its complacent rut. First, however, you should ascertain how much change the customer really wants. Risk tolerance often appears to be greater than it is.

Next, consider bringing in a graphic artist to work with the team. Often, creating a visual image of the process or technology—something that your team will have to do anyway—stimulates new thinking.

Many resources exist to help you promote creativity and innovative thinking. A lot of content on the *Harvard Business Review* website is free or available at a very reasonable cost. You might want to start with an interesting **interview on harnessing creativity** (http://goo.gl/eyo9Ks).

I can also recommend the exercises and processes in *101 Design Methods: A Structured Approach for Driving Innovation in Your Organization* by Vijay

Kumar. To implement these concepts, you will probably need to introduce a new person into the team to facilitate one or more sessions until you get the ball rolling. If you have access to an organizational development professional in your company, consult that person for ideas and suggestions as to how to generate new ideas.

The point is to shake things up rather than expect the behavior of the team to change on its own. Good luck, and think about sharing your experiences in an article or blog post when you are done because a lot of other proposal managers struggle with this issue.

All the best,

Wendy Frieman, The Proposal Doctor

Insights
Capture & Proposal Insights and Tips – Volume 2

Ask the Proposal Doctor

How to screen and interview proposal managers?

Dear Proposal Doctor,

My organization is woefully short of proposal managers, and I have been under pressure to hire more. We advertise in the usual places and we get applicants.

The interview process does not seem to be a good predictor of who will be effective and who will be a good fit with our environment. No matter what questions we ask, we don't seem to find out the right information. Sometimes we are pleasantly surprised; more often, we are not. This means we might be actually turning away the candidates we should be hiring.

What are the right questions to ask? I am wondering how other people screen applicants for this position?

–Immersed in Job Interviews

Dear Immersed,

You are correct. Proposal management is not a textbook subject, so it is difficult to ask "the right" questions. People can claim to have certain skills and attitudes, and they might really believe that they do, without having to prove it on the spot.

There are several different ways to attack the problem. First, if there are specific skills that you require, you can ask the applicant to demonstrate the skills on the spot. Provide a document to format or a formatted document for comment. If you need someone with graphics skills, ask them to render a hand-drawn sketch. You might give the applicant an RFP and ask for a draft schedule or outline. If the applicant gets nervous or balks at this idea, you can be pretty sure you have the wrong person. A truly confident professional loves a challenge like that.

Beware, however. Some HR departments frown on this kind of approach because it smacks too much of a *test*, and tests can, in theory, handicap some minorities. If you are not allowed to administer a test, and even if you are, I would recommend describing the types of specific proposal challenges that occur in your environment and asking the applicant about a recommended approach.

For example, you could ask the proposal manager for some suggested courses of action when there are conflicting opinions on the technical solution. Pick specific scenarios that occur in your organization. Emphasize that there is no one right answer. You will know pretty quickly if the person has the level of sophistication and experience you are looking for. You will also be able to tell something about style and attitude by the way the person responds—and you might get some good ideas in the process.

At the end of the day, it's still a roll of the dice. I have had people turn on a dime in the heat of the moment and become borderline psychotic. I hope that doesn't happen to you! And you probably can't predict that, no matter what questions you ask.

All the best,

Wendy Frieman, The Proposal Doctor

Ask the Proposal Doctor

Pressing commitments – how to be "fair" as proposal manager?

Dear Proposal Doctor,

I am running a big proposal. Several people on the team are critical to the effort because of how much they know. Each seems to have some kind of personal commitment that cuts into their day several times a week. It's either kids, medical appointments, other professional commitments, a sick relative, a household repair, or something else.

I don't want to have one standard for most of the team (you need to be in the office) and another standard for a select minority (you can set your own schedule because I can't live without you).

I am at a loss as to how to manage this and still maintain the morale of the team. Please help.

–Trying To Be Fair

Insights
Capture & Proposal Insights and Tips – Volume 2

Dear Trying,

You are correct. It is very difficult to have two standards and maintain your integrity as a leader.

So, I would suggest just one standard, which is the one I use on all the proposals I manage. Everyone on the team should be able to deal with pressing personal commitments. Proposals can go on for a long time, and we can't turn off the outside world.

On the proposals I have worked, people have died, people have been born, companies have merged, people have had their homes destroyed by floods, kids have graduated from college, relatives have gotten married (and divorced), and on and on and on. Stuff is going to happen.

Notice I said *pressing* personal commitments. For the system to work, everyone has to agree on what constitutes a pressing commitment. Playing golf on Thursday afternoon is not a pressing commitment. Anything connected to health is a pressing commitment in my book. No proposal is worth getting sick or injured. Anything connected to family is pressing. No proposal is worth a divorce, a separation, or an estranged relative.

At the same time, if someone has so many pressing commitments that he or she cannot attend required meetings or keep up with the proposal deadlines, you will need to think about how to redefine and realign roles. Proposals are about teamwork, and sometimes work can be split among several people, or it can be done in shifts— assuming you have a way to do a clean hand-off at the end of a shift.

Instead of changing the standard for one person, change the nature of that person's involvement. That way you can maintain a single standard, and you don't have to feel responsible for keeping someone from a personal commitment.

All the best,

Wendy Frieman, The Proposal Doctor

Insights
Capture & Proposal Insights and Tips – Volume 2

Ask the Proposal Doctor

Do I have to understand the proposal contents as the proposal manager?

Dear Proposal Doctor,

Do I have to actually understand what is in the proposal I am managing? Sometimes this is an overwhelming task, and it distracts me from the blocking and tackling of the day-to-day management.

Often the material is technical and written for people who are "inside the bubble" and who understand all the jargon and acronyms. This makes it difficult to know if the writing is not persuasive or if it is intrinsically not understandable to a layperson. Yet it is hard to give direction to the writers if I don't know anything about the content.

How do others manage this challenge?

–Struggling to Keep Up

Dear Struggling,

This is a constant challenge, and you will be disappointed—or relieved—to know that there is no one-size-fits-all answer.

There is no question that we are better proposal managers when we have a grasp of the subject matter. It helps us get clarity from our contributors and keep them from writing to a narrow audience or assuming too much knowledge on the part of the evaluators. Sometimes that good grasp is just out of reach. Several years ago, I managed a highly technical proposal that weighed in at over 500 pages. A number of people working on it had PhDs. There was no way that I could really understand all of it, and I didn't spend much time trying.

How much time and energy to invest in understanding the subject is going to depend on how much lead-time we have and how much access we have to the SMEs who create all this complicated stuff. Here are several strategies that might help.

First, on the really big ones (I mean with page counts of 1,000 pages or more), limit your involvement in the substance to the high-level outline. Unless you have several years to read into it, or you have been a practitioner in the field being proposed, you will drive yourself crazy trying to understand all the content.

Second, if you have a draft RFP in advance and you have time to prepare, ask the capture manager or the SMEs to explain the solution to you in layman's terms so that you know what to look for. Then read and understand as much as you can without losing sight of the bigger picture and all the logistics.

Third, if you can't understand the content, make sure that someone you trust (capture manager, solution architect) does.

Fourth, if the proposal is short and not highly technical, I recommend getting heavily involved in the content so that you understand all the major sections and the content of the figures and tables. If the team can't explain that information to you in this context, it probably means that they don't understand the material themselves.

In short, context is everything. Assess what makes sense in each situation, knowing that the more content you understand, the better.

All the best,

Wendy Frieman, The Proposal Doctor

Ask the Proposal Doctor

Beyond proposal burnout – what to do?

Dear Proposal Doctor,

With only 2 weeks before a major proposal submittal, the key people on my team are in an advanced state of burn out. Some are sleeping on couches in the office rather than going home. Others come in to work not having slept at all.

It's impossible to move any deadlines and still get the proposal done, and it's going to be impossible to meet the deadlines given the level of exhaustion. Because of multiple proposal extensions, this situation has been intensifying for the last 3 weeks.

It's getting to me as well, since I am ultimately responsible for the final product.

–Beyond Burnout

Dear Beyond,

Many proposal managers have been in your situation. Most fail to demonstrate what your team needs urgently at this moment: leadership.

Insights

Understanding that you do not want to move any deadlines, you must realize that continuing on the current path is dangerous. Someone falling asleep at the office is likely to introduce errors that you won't have the time or energy to catch later. Furthermore, it's one thing to fall asleep at the office, and it's another thing to fall asleep on the road. Exhaustion has been shown to be more dangerous than alcohol for driver safety.

Here is what I recommend:

- Acknowledge the state of the team so that everyone realizes you know that there is a problem and you are dealing with it. As a proposal manager, you should communicate every turning point in the proposal, and you are definitely at one now.

- Give the key players at least 24 hours off and adjust interim deadlines to accommodate a day off. I know this sounds impossible, but a day of rest will increase productivity in a way that can't be imagined from your current state. No amount of effort can compensate for lack of sleep. People who don't exercise every day think that it is too time-consuming; those who do know that regular exercise actually saves more time than it takes because of the increase in energy level. The same is true of adequate sleep.

- Consider re-assigning people, introducing new players, or finding other ways to balance the load. When people are staying up all night to get their work done, they are often in the wrong role. Do the key contributors have what they need to get the work done (equipment, data, connectivity, templates, graphics support)?

- After the day off, formally acknowledge that you are entering a new phase with revised deadlines, schedules, and roles.

Be sure to take care of yourself and don't let yourself get exhausted. Leading by example is critical.

I know you can turn this situation around and wish you all the best,

Wendy Frieman, The Proposal Doctor

Insights
Capture & Proposal Insights and Tips – Volume 2

Ask the Proposal Doctor
Fed up with proposal politics?

Dear Proposal Doctor,

My proposal has become a hornet's nest. The capture manager is intensely unpopular. She makes arbitrary and often unwise decisions with zero transparency. People have to go behind her back to get her decisions reversed because she will not engage in discussion.

Although this could be a unifying force, instead the proposal team has broken up into factions, each trying to curry favor with senior management in an effort to get the capture manager replaced with a candidate of choice. The amount of politicking is mind-boggling. It is no wonder that no one is able to meet any proposal deadlines—they are all too busy plotting and scheming.

It's a demoralizing atmosphere, needless to say, all the more so because the behavior makes it less and less likely that we can win.

As a proposal manager, my power is limited. Yet I am dying to do something to change the atmosphere and get people working productively. What do you suggest?

–Fed Up With Politics

Dear Fed Up,

I would be disgusted and demoralized myself in such a situation. And it is true that as the proposal manager, your power is limited—in theory. In practice, for the team to win, you have to be able to do your job. That means you have leverage.

Right now, there are impediments getting in the way of you doing your job. Don't try to fix the behavior of all the people plotting the palace coup—go to the underlying cause: the capture manager.

You didn't say what your relationship with the capture manager is, so I wonder if you can have a discussion with her in which you point this out. She probably already knows what is going on, but if she doesn't, it might knock some sense into her. Even if you don't have a good relationship with her, you need to have some kind of discussion with her before proceeding to my next recommended step, which is to escalate.

I cannot tell you whom to escalate to because I don't know your organization. You must find someone who will understand how destructive her behavior is and someone who has the power to do something about it. Approach this person as someone who wants to win, which means getting the proposal back on course, which is only possible if the team is united behind an effective leader. Keep the tone objective and professional.

It can be daunting to go over someone's head, but if you have already talked to her, what do you have to lose? By your own admission, you cannot win by continuing the current course of action. Screw up your courage, and do what is right, even if it isn't easy.

All the best,

Wendy Frieman, The Proposal Doctor

Insights

Capture & Proposal Insights and Tips – Volume 2

Ask the Proposal Doctor

How to escape from proposal scheduling hell?

Dear Proposal Doctor,

I am in scheduling hell. Three proposal managers and a proposal coordinator have vacations planned in the next 2 months. All four need the time off, and all four have already postponed vacations in anticipation of upcoming RFPs (none of which arrived on schedule).

Commercial and government customers alike plan to issue an RFP on a certain date and then encounter roadblocks that result in delays of up to a year. How can I plan effectively and still give my staff the time off that they need?

–Struggling with Scheduling

Dear Struggling,

Thanks for your excellent question. In all honesty, this is why I am thrilled to be a single practitioner again and not a manager. There is no silver bullet or easy solution to your problem, which is headache-making for managers in this business.

My approach is radical and it might not work for everyone—before you decide, hear me out.

I don't postpone vacations or trips or occasions for pending RFPs (ongoing proposals are a different story; we can deal with that in another letter). When I commit to a family event, I honor that commitment even if I have a high level of confidence that an RFP will appear that day. In my household, we celebrate birthdays on the actual birthday, anniversaries on the actual date, Passover on whatever night it actually occurs (even though it would be so much more convenient to *move* it to a weekend). You get the idea.

I came to this approach after realizing that dates and commitments are what give meaning to my life, and it undermines my sense of order to start moving them in anticipation of something that might or might not happen—usually, not.

Now, back to your problem. To implement this approach, you need to be prepared in case an RFP does appear when some of your staff is gone. The idea here is to make sure that people and facilities are accessible during the period that your staff will be gone, which is smart planning, and not try to work out all the details until you actually have the paper in your hand. To do more would be over-planning.

Can you cross train? Can you pull in people from another part of the organization to be on call? Can you stagger vacations so that two of the four will always be there? Can you engage outside help on a contingency basis? This means going to your management and laying out a plan that covers the most likely contingencies and, yes, it might mean asking for more money. The investment will pay back in the long run.

Everyone knows someone who seems to have endless energy and sleep 5 hours a night. Research has shown that these people are not as productive as they think they are and not nearly as productive as they could be if they were to sleep more and play more. Once you buy in to this approach, it is amazing how creative you will be in developing ways to implement it.

All the best,

Wendy Frieman, The Proposal Doctor

Ask the Proposal Doctor

What to do with proposal "graphics and mayonnaise" complainers?

Dear Proposal Doctor,

Managing a big, complicated proposal is hard enough without having to listen to my complainers all day. I have two of them. They complain about everything from the quality of the graphics to the mayonnaise on the sandwiches at lunch. Responding to their issues and listening to them vent is just taking too much of my time, and I am worried about meeting our deadline for Red Team. I might even have to postpone it. How can I deal with these individuals?

–Sick and Tired

Dear Sick,

I guess you didn't see the column I wrote on proposal archetypes. The complainer exhibits many of the behaviors of the martyr and the talker, and probably the worst of both.

Here are two principles to keep in mind. First, forget responding to their specific complaints. The complaints are symptoms of an underlying attitude problem. If you improve the mayonnaise, they will start complaining about the mustard. If you hire a better graphics person, they will start complaining about the desktop publishing. Removing a source of dissatisfaction does not create satisfaction.

Second, consider the aptitude/attitude matrix:

The mistake that almost all first-time managers make is to spend their time with people in the lower left quadrant, when they should be

Insights

spending their time with people in the upper right quadrant.

With these principles in mind, where do your two Bobsey twins fit? We already know they are not in either of the two upper boxes. If they are in the bottom right box, which is to say that they are producing valuable content, then is it worth coaching them individually so that they are aware of the effects of their behavior?

It isn't just about your time. Complainers sap the energy and enthusiasm of the entire team, and with two of them feeding on each other, you could have a serious morale meltdown if you don't nip this problem in the bud.

There are plenty of creative ways for complainers to get things off their chest. You can create a space on the electronic Team Site, on the proposal wall, in a journal, on suggestion cards. They can have a 5-minute time slot each day to complain to one other person (preferably someone not on the proposal team). Or, you could counsel them to exercise some self control until the proposal is done, after which they can complain to anyone who is willing to listen. On one proposal, we had a box on the table for the whiners: each whine carried a $5 price tag.

If your twins are in the bottom left box, it is time to replace them. No matter who takes their place, you won't be worse off than you are now. And then, make sure you start paying attention to the people in the upper right quadrant. They are the ones who need your attention, recognition, and reinforcement.

Just as an aside, it always amuses me to hear proposal managers complain. When I hear a proposal manager complain about lack of sleep, pressure, too much to do, etc., I always want to ask them why they are in this profession. Complaining appears to be an American tradition, and it is something we excel at. That doesn't mean that it is admirable or productive.

All the best,

Wendy Frieman, The Proposal Doctor

Insights

Capture & Proposal Insights and Tips – Volume 2

Ask the Proposal Doctor

Why show up if everyone else wants to run the proposal show?

Dear Proposal Doctor,

All of a sudden, everyone on my team is obsessed with fonts and kerning and other aspects of desktop publishing. People who should be worried about the solution and the price are weighing in on the appearance of the document. Everyone has an opinion on the best color scheme, margins, headers, footers, and text boxes.

Isn't this my domain? Shouldn't I have the final say on this? Why is everyone else trying to do my job? What is the point of my showing up for this proposal if everyone else wants to take control of these decisions?

–Feeling Powerless

Dear Feeling,

First, you are not powerless. One of my favorite quotations is from Eleanor Roosevelt, "No one can make you feel inferior without your permission." You can—and should—do three things.

First, as the proposal manager, it is fair that you ask for a meeting to clarify roles and responsibilities with your management chain. At that meeting, you can point out that decisions about the appearance of the document should be made by people with subject matter knowledge on the topic of document layout. No one would let a desktop publisher develop a pricing strategy. No one would accept the opinion of a contracts specialist on how to write a resume.

Each member of a proposal team brings specialized knowledge—and that of desktop publishing and proposal management professionals should be respected to the same degree that we respect the knowledge of solution architects. Based on that logic, the decision should be back in your court. If others want to express an opinion, that is their right. It doesn't mean you have to listen to it or accept it.

Second, work with the desktop publishing expert in your organization (maybe that means you) to identify some external sources of expertise on this topic. Pick a respected source. It could be a style manual from a professional association or a research article showing how readers respond to certain types of layouts. This will objectify, add validity, and reduce the likelihood of opposition.

Insights

Capture & Proposal Insights and Tips – Volume 2

It is much harder to refute a respected source than it is to argue about someone's opinion.

Third, establish a template based on that external source as the default format going forward. Then you can adjust, as required, to each RFP.

Finally, to address your question as to why others want to weigh in on fonts and margins, all I can say is that this is a great way for them to avoid doing their work. I believe it was Hemingway who said that whenever he faced a blank page on his typewriter, he had an insurmountable urge to clean his refrigerator. You can—and must—take back control. Courage!

All the best,

Wendy Frieman, The Proposal Doctor

War Stories

How experts got involved in capture and proposals – and what keeps them coming back—Part 1

Beth Wingate

Ask anyone working in the capture or proposal profession how they got started in this *crazy* business, and you'll get a different answer every time.

There's often an underlying theme in each response, though—most folks never intended to become a capture/proposal professional.

Once someone becomes immersed in this profession, however, a number of factors keep them coming back for more *excitement* year after year.

I asked a number of colleagues how they got started in capture/proposals—and what keeps them coming back for more. Here are their responses.

- It was a necessity to grow my company. It's swim or sink in the federal business. Over time I realized that to grow, we need to be A+ at capture/proposal, so it has become our #2 priority—only behind serving our customers. *–Hamid Moinamin, President, Inserso*

- A friend of a friend asked if I was available to develop graphics on a large proposal. I said, "Yes"—even though I didn't know what a proposal was. We worked crazy hours and ate a lot of delivery. In the end, we helped deliver an amazing product. I returned home tired and weak from lack of sleep. One week later I found that I missed the faster-than-normal pace and interdependence needed to deliver a proposal, so I volunteered to help again. Flash forward 14+ years and I love what I do for the following reasons: I am challenged every day; I get to pursue becoming a guru in our industry; I have relative autonomy; my work has purpose bigger than myself (I get to work with teams and help others achieve their goals);

and I make enough money that I don't worry about money. *–Mike Parkinson, APMP Fellow and Principal, 24 Hour Company*

- I've never been one to think INSIDE the box, and love to know the *why* of things, so competitive intelligence was a natural fit— and every day, I get to study a new technology, or a new approach, or a new strategy, or a new... It's fun, it's intellectually stimulating, and it's profitable! *–Randy Richter, President, Richter & Company*

- For those of us who enjoy creating documents, the proposal world offers the motivation to deliver the most effective documents we can with every competition. And, being part of a winning team several times a year is extremely gratifying, especially when the work is for the benefit of the country. *–David C. Hilnbrand, Principal Consultant, DC Proposal Services and Lohfeld Consulting Group Consultant*

- I learn something new every day. *–Brenda Crist, APMP Fellow and Principal Consultant, Lohfeld Consulting Group*

- I *fell in* from several senior operations
  assignments in which the primary concern
  is always, "How do we win the recompete?" and "How can we use this
  experience to expand into other
  opportunities?" What has kept me coming
  back is the challenge inherent in matching
  my client's capabilities to the target
  opportunity and helping to frame a
  convincing and competitive *winning*
  response. *–Maury Sweetin, Capture
  Manager/Proposal Manager/Red Team
  Captain/Volume Lead, Lohfeld Consulting
  Group*

- I started as an artist because I heard you
  could make more money if you could do
  proposal art (I was a starving artist at the
  time, so *more* sounded good—regardless of
  the hours). I worked my way up through
  the ranks (coordinator, proposal manager,
  director of proposals, orals coach) because I
  love the proposal cycle—beginning,
  middle, end. Well, sometimes throw an
  extension in there. I was very fortunate to
  be able to support and watch many of the
  best orals coaches in the business and how
  their teams reacted to them. I keep coming

back because I love making a difference in people's lives and their wallets. Coaching and managing proposals allows me to do both. *–Ben Rowland, Orals Coach and Lohfeld Consulting Group Consultant*

- I woke up one day and realized that all my best friends and most valued professional contacts were people I had worked with on proposals. It is still true to this day. *–Wendy Frieman, APMP Fellow and Principal Consultant, Lohfeld Consulting Group*

How experts got involved in capture and proposals – and what keeps them coming back—Part 2

Beth Wingate

"How did you get started in capture/proposals?" is a question often asked when meeting new colleagues at a conference, seminar, meeting, or around a war room conference table.

Answers vary from person to person and company to company, but most often practitioners became "accidental" capture or proposal professionals and discovered they love the excitement, colleagues, and "thrill of victory."

I asked a number of colleagues from small to large businesses how they got started in capture/proposals—and what keeps them coming back for more. Here are their responses.

- I fell into proposals when I was a programmer years ago. The company

found out that I could write well and asked me to contribute to the technical approach on a proposal. As I moved from programmer to technical lead to project manager to program manager and finally director, I have continued to gain experience with capture and proposals as part of my other responsibilities. When I *retired*, I decided that I wanted to continue to work in a consulting capacity, and proposal management was a great fit. What keeps me coming back proposal after proposal and year after year is that I always learn something new when I work a proposal and that keeps it exciting.
–*Margie Regis, Proposal Manager, Management Resources Group and Lohfeld Consulting Group Consultant*

- I continue to learn something new every day, and it's never dull!
  –*Kristin Pennypacker, Vice President, Proposal & Capture Management, Planned Systems International*

- I chose this career because it fits me like a glove. I love the intellectual stimulation of working on a wide variety of subject matter; the rigor and discipline of creating

compliant bids; the pleasure of working with many of America's best companies and with bright, interesting, hard-working subject matter experts; and the sense of concrete achievement that comes from turning in a good proposal and, more often than not, of winning. What's not to like?!
–Marty Williamson, Proposal Manager and Lohfeld Consulting Group Consultant

- My first post-MBA job was as a system analyst for a large system integrator (AMS now CGI). After a year or so, I discovered that managing a team of DB2 programmers was not for me. My manager thought I had good writing skills and encouraged me to assist with proposal writing. We won the first proposal I worked on. A number of successful proposals followed in the manufacturing, association, and telecommunications industries. I eventually ran capture and proposal for a blockbuster pursuit that led to one of the largest contracts in the history of the company. A few years later, Deloitte Consulting hired me to grow their telecommunications practice. It was a dream job with a high profile, high pay, big bonuses, and a fancy office. Unfortunately, I was the first director/partner laid off as a result of the telecom industry crash.

It took a number of years to recover from the crushing blow of being laid off from a dream job. With luck, timing, and hard work, I ended up starting my own successful company. As I look back over the years, the Deloitte Consulting layoff was a blessing in disguise. The variety of customers, solutions, people, work locations, schedule flexibility, and compensation make it easy to come back for more every single day. –*Chris Simmons, APMP Fellow and Principal, Rainmakerz Consulting*

- I had worked on bids as a program and product manager, and it was a logical next step to get out of product management. I did not know until 3 months later that I was going to LOVE the work. I love the fast pace, the continuous learning about the products and services, and that every project has a beginning, middle, and end.

Celebrating the wins with the teams keeps me coming back! –*Deborah Brooks, Sr. Bid Manager, TATA Communications*

- I was a line program manager who could write—and folks just kept asking me to work proposals. When I decided I needed a change, my firm moved me to a team that was institutionalizing capture and proposal processes to help build the corporate processes. I just love the strategy, the challenge of winning, and the adrenalin associated with getting a proposal through the process. –*Brooke Crouter, Principal Consultant, Lohfeld Consulting Group*

Insights

How experts got involved in capture and proposals – and what keeps them coming back—Part 3

Beth Wingate

Exciting! Maddening! Crazy! Insane! Appalling! Rewarding! Challenging!

No—not Monday Night Football or five people in the kitchen at once in my house—the capture and proposals world!

In this wrap-up to my 3-part series on why anyone would get involved in this profession—much less stick around for decades and encourage others to join—my industry colleagues share their stories about how they fell into their capture/proposal careers and what keeps them coming back for more.

- I fell into proposals because I was a degreed engineer who could also write grammatically correct English—a rare commodity to this day. I keep coming back for more because I like to WIN, plus I enjoy working fast-paced projects (I tell people that I have a short attention span). I like to see my *product*—the winning proposal—at the end of an assignment. I enjoy the wide variety of acquisitions, technologies, and services that I work on. I like working with smart people who do good work and are willing to learn from me, an outside consultant. *–Pat Cosimano, Owner of Pat Cosimano Wins and Lohfeld Consulting Group Consultant*

- Proposal writing was not my first career choice, but, as it turns out, suits me well. Following graduate school, I was an analyst for an environmental consultancy. When my division folded as a result of a lost proposal effort, management created a dedicated proposal group and retained me as its manager/writer/coordinator. They supported my Shipley training and APMP membership (and I enthusiastically became an active member, serving as the Northeast Communications Director from 1994–1997 and then as President in 1997–1998), and gave me any and all tools I needed to build a strong center. I never returned to my former position. Over the years, I changed companies and continued to gain valuable proposal writing experience until I branched out on my own as a contractor. Proposal work plays to my strengths: I love writing, and the challenges inherent in writing persuasive, concise proposals that meet RFP requirements; I enjoy collaborating with team members in telling a well-organized, succinct *story* that convinces evaluators this client is clearly the only choice; and lastly, I'm fiercely competitive and find real satisfaction in helping my clients win. *–Luanne Smulsky, Principal, ib4e Writing Solutions and Lohfeld Consulting Group Consultant*

- I was a junior management consultant, and my boss asked me to help write a proposal. He liked what he saw and got me involved in a lot of bids. I enjoy the profession because every proposal is a puzzle that I enjoy working out. *–Lisa Pafe, Principal Consultant, Lohfeld Consulting Group*

- I fell into proposal management by being in the right place at the right time. The proposal manager made a fatal mistake by

shipping a proposal to the U.S. Postal Service via FedEx, which the customer informed our team never to do again. The next day the proposal manager packed his bags and went elsewhere. The opening existed, and I was offered the job.
–Betsy Blakney, APMP Fellow and Director of Proposal Management, CACI

- After 10 years of editing, I was burned out; however, I wanted to continue working in a proposal-related career because I enjoy the pace, the variety of projects, and the people—so I started formatting (desktop publishing) and I haven't looked back. To me formatting is like working on a puzzle. The proposal comes to me in pieces (e.g., various sections) and, based on RFP requirements and client needs, I create a cohesive, compliant document that is esthetically pleasing. Seeing all of the pieces come together with a consistent look across all volumes is truly satisfying.
–Mary Beth Frazza, Owner, Frazza Formatting and Lohfeld Consulting Group Consultant

- I really like working with smart people and always found myself drawn to the more creative ends of the business. Capture and proposal work is the forum for applying technology and management creativity. In these roles, you are always challenging the status quo to find a better way to deliver more value in the solutions and services you propose. I liked conceptualizing and writing about better ways to do the work for our customers. I also liked the op temp of these activities—lots of hard work that resulted in a proposal that everyone could be proud of. *–Bob Lohfeld, APMP Fellow and CEO, Lohfeld Consulting Group*

Industry experts' proposal war stories and lessons learned— Part 1

Beth Wingate

We've all heard the war stories around the office coffee pot and at industry events and cringed, thinking, "Wow! I'll make sure that NEVER happens to one of my proposal efforts."

There are as many potential disasters waiting out there, however, as there are RFPs in the Cloud— and I'm sure we'd all rather learn from someone else's horror story than become the originator of a *classic* ourselves!

I asked a number of my colleagues to share their favorite war stories—and to tell us what they learned from the experience.

- I was in an organization that decided to bid on a job where we did not know the customer, the customer did not know us, a well-loved incumbent was in place, we only had a 75% solution for performing the job, and our solution was high-risk operationally. The bid process rocked the organization, resulting in massive dissension. The moral of the story is do not delude yourself. Put a bid qualification process in place that is objective, generates solutions that meet the customer's business objectives, enables you to differentiate yourself from the competitors, and results in a high-quality proposal that can be produced on schedule within an acceptable level of risk. –*Brenda Crist, APMP Fellow and Principal Consultant, Lohfeld Consulting Group*

- Most memorable are the ones that involve inadequate advance planning. Here's an example. While an Operations VP at JPL, our company decided to team with a small firm to meet the small business (SB) constraints. *Small* turned out to be an understatement. As prime, they insisted that they should prepare the proposal in their facility in Orange County, about 50 miles from the delivery office, although we had all necessary facilities within walking distance of the customer. Delivery day came and was met by a huge traffic jam on the freeways, a bank robbery near Pasadena, and a SNAFU in prime production. Their rep called us about 6 hours prior to the deadline and announced that, due to the traffic problems, they were hiring a helicopter to make the delivery. Our mission was to *find* a landing spot and remain in communication via then-primitive cell phone so as to meet and deliver the prop. We never heard from them again and couldn't find an authorized landing spot. We missed the delivery deadline for the only time during my career of arriving on time at least 20 times. Moral: plan ahead, keep it simple, and leave time for catastrophes. *–Maury Sweetin, Capture Manager/Proposal Manager/Red Team Captain/Volume Lead, Lohfeld Consulting Group*

- I read a question submitted on a major procurement that had obviously been reviewed to death before it was submitted—obviously, because it contained parenthetical comments from reviewers, including the comment, "Whose stupid requirement was this anyway?" The

government provided a detailed response, including (in parentheses), "By the way, as the Contracting Officer, it was my stupid requirement." Lesson learned: questions are only effective if properly posed—and carefully reviewed prior to submittal.
–*Randy Richter, President, Richter & Company*

- I once had a program manager from the Bronx named Tony. He had a thick accent and hired a speech pathologist to remove it before orals day. With more than $300M at stake, Tony did not think his accent would play well in Richmond, VA—which he considered the center of the deep south. It was his greatest weakness he told me. I was brought in late as an orals coach and immediately asked Tony to lose the speech pathologist and work with me to make his accent his greatest asset. It took some persuasion, but Tony agreed and additionally agreed to craft the first minute of his presentation and practice it daily 20 times. It went something like this in a very thick accent. "Hello, my name is Tony and I am from the Bronx, New York. I am the program manager and will be leading you through the next few days. The first thing I would like you to know is that my company has generously offered to provide translations services for anyone requiring them (said with an extra thick accent)." At that point, the reviewers began to roar with laughter and a few of them laughingly yelled out in deep southern accents, "You might need some this way too!" Everybody laughed. But more than that, over the next few days everybody tried their Bronx accent and their deep south accent—and others. It became the lighthearted introduction to any conversation on the stage and in the hallway. It became bigger than Tony, the company, the orals, and the solicitation—it was just good fun that brought people together. It was an unusual orals—3 days long with over 50 reviewers in the room at any one time. Tony had done it. His company won the bid, and nobody will ever forget him. But, I got the real prize. I learned that perceived weaknesses are just that—perceived. They are not real and can even be used as strengths. It's a choice—not a condition. *–Ben Rowland, Orals Coach and Lohfeld Consulting Group Consultant*

Insights
Capture & Proposal Insights and Tips – Volume 2

- *Deliver the car!* is best proposal story I know. Many years ago a proposal was being delivered in the trunk of a car. The delivery car was in an accident. With minutes remaining until delivery cutoff, the trunk was crushed closed and would not open. A frantic call to the boss was made. The boss exclaimed, "Deliver the car!" (In the end, the car trunk was forced open and the proposal was delivered on time.) I learned to always plan ahead, have a backup plan, and be flexible.
  –Mike Parkinson, APMP Fellow and Principal, 24 Hour Company (Note: Marilyn Moldovan shared this story with us at an APMP conference years ago—it's become an industry classic! *–Beth Wingate, Managing Director, Lohfeld Consulting Group*)

Industry experts' proposal war stories and lessons learned— Part 2

Beth Wingate

We've all heard, "The definition of insanity is doing the same thing over and over again and expecting different results." (–Albert Einstein) Has this quote applied to any capture or proposal efforts you've supported?

I've heard war stories and observed some first-hand over the past 25 years that make me wonder how some capture and proposal folks simply haven't learned from their own and others' mistakes and broken the constant cycle of self-sabotage.

I asked a number of my colleagues to share some of their favorite war stories—and tell us what they learned from their experiences. Here is part 2 of my 4-part series on capture and proposal war stories.

Insights
Capture & Proposal Insights and Tips – Volume 2

- There have been many wars, death marches, battles, and skirmishes through the years. Most of the war stories stem from not using a defined proposal process, and as the process matures and even small companies have come to embrace it, the wars have become fewer and less painful. A few years ago, I was called as a consultant to a large company to do a Pink Team review and be part of the tiger team going forward. The Pink Team version of the proposal consisted of an outline and large amounts of text from previous proposals that had been cut and pasted into the proposal—there were no storyboards, no solution, no themes, and no semblance of compliance. Needless to say, the entire proposal was thrown out and we started over. Again, the Proposal Manager did not apply the process, and the next version was better in some areas, but at Red Team (1 week before it was due), it was still far off the mark even in the area of compliance. As luck would have it, as we were developing the post-Red Team get-well plan, we received a 2-week extension. It was a rough 2 weeks, but through hard work and a lot of long hours we were able to pull together a winning proposal. Process matters…ignore it at your own risk. *–Margie Regis, Proposal Manager, Management Resources Group and Lohfeld Consulting Group Consultant*

- I managed a great proposal, and we still lost. There were numerous post-mortems, and everyone agreed that the document was excellent. The program manager on site with the customer had generated too much ill will. No matter what was in the proposal, the customer would have changed contractors, and we would have lost. This taught me that there are limits to what I can control and that I will always be in a box. The challenge is to do the best job I can inside the box. *–Wendy Frieman, APMP Fellow and Principal Consultant, Lohfeld Consulting Group*

- Our company had the good fortune of helping a commercial division of a large system integrator win their first large government contract (a $3B blanket purchase agreement). We were originally hired to review the first draft of the proposal. After the review, it became clear to the customer that the proposal was in big trouble. It wasn't compliant, had major solution gaps, lacked differentiating themes, had virtually no graphics, you name it. The customer needed help, but no one wanted to take over the proposal management and writing functions—not even one of the largest and most reputable consulting firms in our industry. They thought it was impossible to win. We agreed to take on the assignment simply because a valued customer needed help. Our team of four consultants was under intense pressure and scrutiny (all the way up to the chairman of the company) to help create a winning proposal in less than 30 days. I never worked harder, longer, or smarter for the next few weeks. During the proposal development process I met the chairman of the company (a national figure) who checked in on us a number of times and offered encouragement and support. Even though our chances of winning were still in doubt, our team had a great sense of accomplishment when we submitted the bid. A few months passed, and the next thing I remember is receiving a congratulatory message from the chairman that we won! Thomas Carlyle, a Scottish essayist, satirist, and historian once said, "No pressure, no diamonds." This quote was popularized by the rookie Washington Redskins quarterback Robert Griffin III and is as true today as it was in the 19th century. This proposal was one of the most difficult and pressure-filled tasks of my career. It was also the most rewarding one. –*Chris Simmons, APMP Fellow and Principal, Rainmakerz Consulting, LLC*

- I worked with a capture manager who crafted a great capture strategy. Unfortunately, it was all in his head—he didn't like to write anything down! Due to a family crisis, he was out of the office for more than 8 weeks. No one had the detailed level of information that we needed to continue positioning us and to send consistent messaging into the client let alone to brief senior management at gate reviews. If it's not written down, it does not exist. –*Kristin Pennypacker, Vice President, Proposal & Capture Management, Planned Systems International*

Industry experts' proposal war stories and lessons learned— Part 3

Beth Wingate

What do two or more capture and proposal folks inevitably talk about when we get together—our latest war stories, of course!

Just like ants and bees go back to their nests and hives and share information with their peers, I think the sharing of war stories at every capture/proposal gathering is some sort of subliminal *survival mechanism* in this profession.

I asked a number of my colleagues to share their favorite war stories—and tell us what they learned from the experience. Here is part 3 of my 4-part series on capture and proposal war stories.

- Over the years we've seen people suffer serious health issues, buildings be struck by lightning, FedEx packages go missing, and weather-related *apocalypses*. The best advice

I can take from all of these is to leave extra time; never ever push final production or delivery until the last minute! *–Colleen Jolly, APMP Fellow and Principal, 24 Hour Company*

- We had a bid that required a significant number of past performance references. The project managers all verified their government Contracting Officer's Representatives (COR) would provide an outstanding reference. We submitted the proposal and got outstanding technical, management, personnel, and cost scores from the client. However, one of the references turned out to be less than stellar and we lost the contract. The moral of this story is to verify that any past performance reference you submit is outstanding and can earn top scores. *–Brenda Crist, APMP Fellow and Principal Consultant, Lohfeld Consulting Group*

- A long, long time ago, I had to ship a proposal to Italy. The FedEx truck in Italy carrying the proposal was hijacked and robbed! We had to get a statement from FedEx to prove the proposal was on the truck and let the customer know!

Fortunately, the customer allowed us to resubmit! Always track the packages and plan for contingencies. *–Deborah Brooks, Sr. Bid Manager, TATA Communications*

- You need to have hobbies and outside interests to balance proposal work: one of mine is quilting. Knowing about the tools and techniques for cutting fabric saved the day on a proposal we did in a small town. It was Friday evening, and the desktop publishing (DTP) lead did not have his normal tools for cutting binder covers and spine inserts for the proposal that was due on Monday. All the local office supply stores had closed for the weekend. I went to the local Walmart and purchased a rotary cutter set intended for cutting fabric for patchwork quilts; showed him how to use the rotary cutter, ruler, and mat; and he successfully cut the cover inserts so that all was ready on Monday morning when we delivered. *–Pat Cosimano, Owner of Pat Cosimano Wins LLC and Lohfeld Consulting Group Consultant*

- Know when to stop. Proposals will fill up all the time available—but you have to know when to stop and allow time to

produce and deliver. My favorite delivery
was one where the contracting officer
waited outside the building for me to sign
the receipt—because the time stamp would
have marked me as late. We let the writers
push the ability to edit and produce—and I
never let that happen again! Now I stop the
writers and do an orderly production.
*–Brooke Crouter, Principal Consultant, Lohfeld
Consulting Group*

Insights

Capture & Proposal Insights and Tips – Volume 2

Industry experts' proposal war stories and lessons learned— Part 4

Beth Wingate

Once more unto the breach, dear friends,
once more;
Or close the wall up with our English dead.
In peace there's nothing so becomes a man
As modest stillness and humility:
But when the blast of war blows in our ears,
Then imitate the action of the tiger;
Stiffen the sinews, summon up the blood...
Now set the teeth and stretch the nostril wide,
Hold hard the breath and bend up every spirit
To his full height.
On, on, you noblest English.
(—William Shakespeare, Henry V, Act III, 1598)

Here's the wrap-up of my 4-part series on capture and proposal war stories shared from industry veterans.

As you engage in your next capture and proposal effort—unto the breach again—consider the war stories shared in my previous articles and those below, and commit to avoiding them in your future engagements.

- The experience from which I learned the most valuable lesson happened early in my career, when I was a very *green* proposal center manager (and lead writer/coordinator as well). The proposal was due at 12:00 p.m. to a state Department of Transportation (DOT). That morning, I was still receiving edits from reviewers and coordinating graphics and word processing. Printing and binding wasn't completed until about 11:00 a.m., so I canceled our courier and held on to the proposal for dear life as our graphic artist sped down the Massachusetts turnpike. Literally jumping out of the moving car, I raced up the escalator to the third floor, pushing past everyone and anyone in my way, only to arrive at the DOT secretary's desk at 12:03 p.m. 12:03 p.m.—3 minutes too late; 180 seconds too late. No amount of cajoling changed her mind (and rightly so)—she could not stamp our proposal. The phone call I made to our VP of Sales/Marketing was the lowest moment of

my young career. I learned the hard way—deadlines are deadlines…period. And, if the client can impose them without exception, then so can the proposal manager. I now build in so much time at the end of proposal schedules that SMEs frequently grumble about their initial draft due dates. Recounting that story is a great way to silence those complaints.
–*Luanne Smulsky, Principal, ib4e Writing Solutions LLC and Lohfeld Consulting Group Consultant*

- A non-native English speaker confused the word *improve* with *improvise,* and informed the customer we were going to *improvise* their processes. No one noticed this error until production. I learned that neither color team reviewers nor spell check catch all errors—a fresh pair of eyes is always useful! –*Lisa Pafe, Principal Consultant, Lohfeld Consulting Group*

- During an orals presentation that was being taped by the government, the videographer dropped to the floor and started crawling under the table pulling on cables. After a few minutes, he got up and went back to recording. During the Q&A session, the contracting officer asked whether or not there was anything that caused the team distress or was a distraction, and the bid program manager responded with a simple *no*. Lesson learned: one doesn't have to repeat the process or implement a *do-over* strategy if one believes it wasn't their problem. *–Betsy Blakney, APMP Fellow and Director of Proposal Management, CACI*

- My favorite proposal-related war story was when, on a beautiful sunny day, the power went out and fried the chargers of three of our five laptops (mine included). Three of us working on one side of the room had our laptops plugged into the same electrical outlet. Unexpected? You bet! Apparently, a car hit a utility box a few blocks away causing a massive outage. Luckily, I had recently saved my work to the external hard drive that I use. What I learned from that experience was to carry an extra charger and to save often to an external hard drive! *–Mary Beth Frazza, Owner, Frazza Formatting and Lohfeld Consulting Group Consultant*

- I worked very hard on a capture and proposal activity for a major NASA bid and thought we had done a good job on it. Apparently the government didn't think so, and when they debriefed us as a losing bidder, they found lots of shortcomings in our bid. After reflecting on the loss, I concluded we should never have bid this deal. It was just too much of a stretch for us to be a credible winner. After that, I had a new appreciation for making good pursuit and bid decisions and raised my personal standards for what deals we would chase. Tightening up our pursuit and bid criteria raised our win rate, reduced our workload, lessened our B&P expenditure, and produced steady revenue growth for the corporation. Looking back at this it all seems so simple. To be a winner, you just have to stop chasing losers. *–Bob Lohfeld, APMP Fellow and CEO, Lohfeld Consulting Group*

Insights
Capture & Proposal Insights and Tips – Volume 2

Advice from Experts

Expert advice for starting out in capture and proposal-related positions

Beth Wingate

I've heard from a number of capture and proposal industry experts who shared their best advice for someone starting out in a capture or proposal-related position, e.g., proposal manager, capture manager, proposal coordinator, graphics, writer, pricer, etc.

Whether you're relatively new to the capture- or proposal-related profession or are a seasoned veteran, there are things you've learned that you can share with all of us that can help us improve our professional and personal management and interpersonal skills, abilities, and focus.

- Acquire an experienced mentor(s) either within your company, a professional association, or a private capture/proposal consulting company. Join the <u>Association of Proposal Management Professionals</u>

(APMP) (www.APMP.org) to obtain access to its large library of information and best practices. Obtain formal training either through reading books, attending classes, or listening to webinars. Review the trade papers to learn more about who is winning in your industry and learn how they differentiate themselves. Implement a standard and repeatable process for capture, proposal, and pricing within your organization that is supported by executives. Acquire and learn how to use tools to expedite proposal schedule management, knowledge management, collaboration, graphics, and configuration management. *–Brenda Crist, APMP Fellow and Principal Consultant, Lohfeld Consulting Group*

- First, take a good course to learn (or solidify your knowledge of) best practices. Next, be an *honest broker* for your client. They deserve our best advice, even when it contradicts internal *conventional wisdom.* *–Maury Sweetin, Capture Manager/Proposal Manager/Red Team Captain/Volume Lead, Lohfeld Consulting Group*

Insights

Capture & Proposal Insights and Tips – Volume 2

- Learn effective time management skills and remove the term *late* from your vocabulary. And remember, a well-fed proposal team is a productive proposal team!
  – *Randy Richter, President, Richter & Company*

- Nothing substitutes for experience. Get training, participate in professional conferences and events, but you will still need to experience numerous proposal cycles before you become competent.
  –*Lisa Pafe, Principal Consultant, Lohfeld Consulting Group*

- Focus on winning. There is a lot that goes into a proposal, and it is easy to lose sight of the goal—winning. Keep your eye on the prize during the proposal storm.
  –*Hamid Moinamin, President, Inserso*

- In general, anyone starting out in proposals would benefit from doing two things: one, approaching everyone they meet (at work, at networking events, etc.) with an eye towards learning and sharing, and two, making sure your family and friends understand the pace and potential stress level of the proposal environment—you will need their support to make proposals your career! –*Colleen Jolly, APMP Fellow and Principal, 24 Hour Company*

- Empathize with your team and client. I find that when I actively seek to understand (e.g., ask questions, listen, research), I get MUCH better results. I attribute a lot of my success as a proposal professional to this approach. Additionally, do what you love. I am passionate about visual communication and it shows. I've been told my enthusiasm is infectious. Doing what I do makes me happy. Good things come from this. –*Mike Parkinson, APMP Fellow and Principal, 24 Hour Company*

- Make compliance your friend. Study it. Learn it. Love it. The most practical experiences that taught me the most were creating proposal outlines where I had to examine the requirements line-by-line and creating compliance matrices that did the same. Truly understanding the requirements will always give you the right response information, language, and tone you need to *answer the mail*. Love compliance to win. *–Ben Rowland, Orals Coach and Lohfeld Consulting Group Consultant*

- Capture and proposals are exciting endeavors, but are fraught with frustrations, so patience and a level head are definite prerequisites for any of these positions. In general, process and organization are key elements in dealing with frustration and keeping your wits about you. That said, my advice to people starting out is to work your way up the ranks and not try to run before you can walk. In other words, the progression from coordinator/writer to volume lead to proposal manager is important for gaining the experience required for success. Knowing the process is important, but in this line of work experience is what gives you the tools for overcoming hurdles and road blocks and the insight that is needed to determine how and when to alter the process to fit the situation. Another tip would be to find a mentor who is willing to share their process and experience with you. For instance, if you are a proposal coordinator and want to move to volume lead or proposal manager, ask the current volume lead/proposal manager to walk you through the process as it unfolds and to explain their techniques for dealing with issues as they arise. *–Margie Regis, Proposal Manager, Management Resources Group and Lohfeld Consulting Group Consultant*

- Select a mentor, someone you can turn to for advice and guidance.
  –Kristin Pennypacker, Vice President, Proposal & Capture Management, Planned Systems International

- Listen. Follow directions. Take constructive criticism well, and use it to your advantage. After 20+ years in this business, I still follow that advice—and am a better proposal writer for doing so. *–Luanne Smulsky, Principal, ib4e Writing Solutions LLC and Lohfeld Consulting Group Consultant*

- Shadow someone who knows what they are doing before diving in cold; align yourself with a mentor. *–Betsy Blakney, APMP Fellow and Director of Proposal Management, CACI*

- The advice I would give to someone starting out in a proposal-related position is to be flexible. A lot has to happen for a proposal to come together, and as a result, deadlines are tight. Any number of things can impact a deadline; changes based on internal reviews or an amendment from the government can change the scope of a proposal. If/when that occurs, the entire team's schedule is impacted, which can create tension. Remaining flexible (and calm) when changes occur eliminates undue stress on the individual and the process as a whole. *–Mary Beth Frazza, Owner, Frazza Formatting and Lohfeld Consulting Group Consultant*

- Get involved and *just do it*. You have to figure out who is good at this and work with them. There is no substitution for practice and experience—and then applying what you learn. I can tell you how to do it—and warn you about pitfalls, but practice will help people dig in. And, do everything you can—every section—so you get experience in multiple areas and in the types of thinking/strategies required for each element of the work. *–Brooke Crouter, Principal Consultant, Lohfeld Consulting Group*

- Get clear definition of your role at a very granular level. This might sound like over-engineering, but it will pay off if everyone has the same expectations as to exactly what you are going to be responsible for and accountable for. Typically, descriptions of roles are written at a high level; this leaves lots of room for different interpretations and expectations.
  –Wendy Frieman, APMP Fellow and Principal Consultant, Lohfeld Consulting Group

- Here's my top-10 list for someone starting out in capture/proposal or any practice area for that matter:

  1. Find your industry niche and your passion

  2. Build trusting relationships (managers, peers, subordinates, customers, partners)

  3. Stay current with new/emerging best practices (accreditation)

  4. Make/take time for yourself

5. Share the credit for your successes, and take responsibility for your failures

6. Take constructive criticism seriously, and learn from your mistakes

7. Give back to your profession

8. Be ethical in everything you do

9. Your customer(s) always come first

10. Work hard and have fun (easy to say…hard to do)
    –Chris Simmons, APMP Fellow and Principal, Rainmakerz Consulting

- Be flexible: master as many different aspects of the business as you can so that you provide the maximum value to your employer or client. *–Pat Cosimano, Owner of Pat Cosimano Wins and Lohfeld Consulting Group Consultant*

- One of the most valuable things I learned during a few years in direct marketing is the importance of verisimilitude, a fun-to-say word that describes the appearance of truth. The yellow note stuck to the sales letter that says, "Chris, check this out!" in

blue cursive ink loses its verisimilitude the moment Chris realizes the handwriting is an electronic font. The realistic movie loses it when the hero jumps out of the helicopter, lands on a log, and rides it down the mountain to safety. And, proposals lose verisimilitude the moment evaluators read, "Our Quality Manager is a stickier for details [sic]," or "Our solution is entirely risk-free," or "We are the leading IT solution provider in the industry."
–David C. Hilnbrand, Principal Consultant, DC Proposal Services and Lohfeld Consulting Group Consultant

- Learn everything you can about the roles and responsibilities of the people who will be on your bid teams. Always be honest with the team and management about the status of the bid you are working on, and escalate whenever you need to. Don't be afraid to say NO to unreasonable requests!
–Deborah Brooks, Sr. Bid Manager, TATA Communications

- These are the positions that are the most fun in corporations because you will work with the company's best and brightest leaders. You will work harder than you have ever worked before, and you must love the challenge to be successful. Learn all that you can about everything you are doing, and always focus on what the customer needs and wants. The one who best understands what the customer wants will likely win. As I like to say, "Best informed wins." –*Bob Lohfeld, APMP Fellow and CEO, Lohfeld Consulting Group*

What advice would you share with someone new (or experienced) in the capture and proposal field?

5 tips to achieve high-performance teams

Lisa Pafe

Crafting solutions is an intellectual challenge, but it is also a team challenge. Whether as part of a bid to win work or a consulting assignment to solve a customer problem, the solution-development process involves a team. Yet, no matter how many masterminds you assemble, the team is often its own worst enemy.

As a team lead, project manager, or proposal manager, how many times have you thought you did everything right? You assemble experts to brainstorm, architect, write, and review…only to result in a non-compelling or even non-compliant solution. With a solution that does not reflect the customer's vision and objectives, what happened?

Let's step back from the solution, and take a look at the team. Project and proposal teams are short-term, often hastily assembled, and face enormous time constraints. People cycle in and out (writers, solution architects, subject matter experts, reviewers). The team members typically offer

Insights
Capture & Proposal Insights and Tips – Volume 2

diverse levels of understanding. Often, some members are remote and/or are at best reluctant participants. They may consider the work low priority and demonstrate a lack of commitment to the team. Team members may show disrespect for the project or proposal manager who is not their line boss. And finally, teams often include teaming partner companies with their own agendas.

These issues could be worked out if you had more time, say 6 months or so. All teams go through five developmental stages that psychologist and educator Bruce Tuckerman identified decades ago: *forming, storming, norming, performing,* and *adjourning (Bruce W. Tuckman, 'Developmental sequence in small groups', Psychological Bulletin, 1965 & 'Developmental sequence in small groups – Current Concerns', 1984).* Subsequent research tells us that three-fifths of team time is taken up by the first two difficult stages.

With typical project or proposal time constraints, your team may have only a week or two to advance to the *performing* stage. Through lessons learned, organizational and group theory, and the school of hard knocks, I've developed some strategies to evolve more efficiently to the *performing* stage.

Insights
Capture & Proposal Insights and Tips – Volume 2

Forming

In the *forming* stage, clarity and communications are paramount. How can you make things clearer? First, ensure the team is clear on the goal. Yes, our team wants to develop a winning solution, but why? Offer a comprehensive vision of what solution development means in terms of strategy, positioning, growth, profitability, and jobs. Often team members avoid asking questions because they don't want to appear uninformed. Why is each team member here? Team members may not know each other. Share with the group each contributor's experience, competencies, role, and responsibilities.

Tip 1: Get off-line. During *forming*, avoid relying solely on team meetings. Spend time off-line with each team member to ensure understanding, and answer questions privately while building rapport. Remember that during the *forming* stage, team members tend to be more polite and hesitant to voice opinions or ask questions. By conversing privately, you can encourage questions, address concerns, and better gauge capabilities.

Storming

Storming is the most challenging stage, but it is necessary in order to *norm*. Differing opinions can create conflicts that lead to anger, confusion, hurt feelings and/or frustration. Exercise authority. Keep team meetings to the point, within time constraints, and follow the agenda, but do ask people to speak up and voice opinions. Respectfully acknowledge issues or conflicts raised and try to resolve them. Continue to remind everyone of the end goal. Avoid getting defensive or taking it personally when team members express frustration or anger. If team members continue fighting and/or straying off topic, call them on it. Create a parking lot for their issues, and address them off-line, one-on-one. In other words, circumvent the team as needed.

Tip 2: Don't get stuck storming. You don't have the luxury of time to work through *storming* at a leisurely pace. Therefore, apply an Agile, iterative approach. Require contributors (individuals or small groups) to submit their assignments daily in small increments so you can provide feedback and coaching. If you see a way another team member can help, get him/her involved. In other words, use *storming* as the pathway to continuously clarify and build a stronger team.

Norming

Norming is when the team members start to become comfortable with their individual roles as part of the group. You've helped them progress by confronting issues, clarifying questions, and coaching poor or struggling performers. Continue to require frequent iterations of work products. Use praise and constructive, actionable criticism as needed. Quite often, a team member or two refuses to *norm*. You may have to remove them from the team if they are disrupting progress.

Tip 3: Anticipate and deal with regression. Be aware that as team members cycle out (after completing a specific assignment) and cycle in (as peer reviewers), the team may regress back to *storming*. You need to apply the same method of working one-on-one with new team members, coaching and clarifying to develop the solution. You also need to gather feedback and lessons learned from the exiting members.

Performing

During the *performing* stage, the team becomes more self-directed. As new members cycle in or out, the team is less likely to regress back to *storming*. Continue to be fair, decisive, in control, and demanding. Ensure work products are on schedule, compliant and compelling, and re-direct the team if they are moving off course.

Tip 4: Exploit both strengths and weaknesses. As the team is now a cohesive unit, team members better understand each other's competencies. Ensure the team is exploiting these—in other words, if someone is better at reviewing the solution than writing, switch roles. Segment competencies so everyone is performing at their peak.

Adjourning

Part of the lessons-learned process includes gathering feedback from each contributor as well as assessing each team member's performance to use in the future when building teams. Record lessons learned on how well these techniques work. These ideas sound easy, but are often difficult to practice and require repeated efforts to perfect.

Tip 5: Don't forget the team. Once the proposal or project is complete, remember to thank team members for their contributions. Inform team members of lessons learned, outcomes, and results to improve individual performance and strengthen future teams.

Looking to the Future

21 Experts' predictions for capture and proposal industry changes—Part 1

Beth Wingate

It's a fact of life that government contracting experiences cyclical changes. Hang around in this game long enough, and you'll start to recognize patterns. Over the last 25+ years, I've seen government contracting shops experience cycles of expansion and contraction, staffed by well-trained professionals and maddeningly inexperienced folks.

I've seen emphasis on best value turn to LPTA. Contracting groups force fitting every procurement they could into performance-based contracts—many of which had no business even being mentioned in the same breath as *performance-based*. Increases and decreases in the number of bid protests and changes in the government offices charged with adjudicating those protests.

Throughout all of these fluctuations and transformations, one thing remains constant. Business development, capture, and proposal professionals have strong opinions about and desires for changes that would add sanity and structure to the entire procurement process and cut down on the *guesswork*.

I asked a number of my colleagues, "What changes do you anticipate in the next 5 years for the capture/proposal industry, e.g., technology and tools, types of proposals, customers, training, lead time to prepare responses, pricing, etc.?" Here are some of their responses. How do their projections match up with yours?

- In the next 5 years, B&P budgets will be tighter, technology innovations will support productivity gains at modest costs, proposal processes will become more agile, proposals will be shorter in length, and capture/proposal personnel will be less specialized and able to do more with less— resulting in more training to close skill gaps. I also think more pricing tools and libraries will become available.
  —Brenda Crist, APMP Fellow and Principal Consultant, Lohfeld Consulting Group

Insights
Capture & Proposal Insights and Tips – Volume 2

- Better use of the *framework*. I believe there will be a serious review of the truisms that are considered current *best practices*. Namely, Black Hats, storyboards, and color reviews have frequently become formulaic milestones, but most often do not encourage evolution of a draft to the final product. Hopefully, our clients, with our encouragement, will begin to apply these tools with more judgment based on the specific parameters of each opportunity. *–Maury Sweetin, Capture Manager/Proposal Manager/Red Team Captain/Volume Lead, Lohfeld Consulting Group*

- The good news: physical proposal rooms will be phased out as managers become more comfortable with virtual proposal technology. The bad news: as more and more government acquisition staff retire, RFP quality will decrease, making proposal work even more *exciting*. (And hopefully, the pendulum will swing back to best value from the current LPTA mindset—or at least, government COs will follow the Federal Acquisition Regulations (FAR) and recognize the correct form to use in solicitations). –*Randy Richter, President, Richter & Company*

- I think the capture/proposal industry will continue to grow. The government is getting more complex by the day, and every day new companies are chasing government work. End result will be crowded space—making the proposal that much more important to stand out. –*Hamid Moinamin, President, Inserso*

- I believe there will continue to be more and more competition for less work. As the government becomes inundated with bids, they will try to make their life easier with more page constraints, challenging proposal professionals to get the message across more succinctly. I also believe that the current LPTA trend will shift back to best value once the government realizes that nothing substitutes for quality. –*Lisa Pafe, Principal Consultant, Lohfeld Consulting Group, Inc.*

- It seems like there will be less money to go around in the future, both in the federal sector as well as in the commercial as the government and businesses tighten their belts. Having a clear, well-written, and well-presented proposal or presentation is going to be even more important in making your company stand out. *–Colleen Jolly, APMP Fellow and Principal, 24 Hour Company*

- I expect to see more remote workers with specialized talents, e.g., resume specialists, past performance specialists, and digital artists. I also expect to see more graphics as mankind's thirst for visuals increases and we *as an industry* get it that pictures sell. A move back to STOP and GO development (Sequential Thematic Organization of Proposals and Graphics Orientation) that was developed by Hughes Aircraft in the mid-60s. *–Ben Rowland, Orals Coach and Lohfeld Consulting Group Consultant*

21 Experts' predictions for capture and proposal industry changes—Part 2

Beth Wingate

The old adage says, "Nothing's constant except change." (We can add death and taxes, but even the taxes part seems in constant flux these days!)

Stay in the government capture and proposal game long enough, and you'll start recognizing patterns in the changes. Over the years, you'll add strategies to your bag of tricks that you'll be able to whip out to deal with round x of a particular procurement *flavor of the year.*

Throughout all of these fluctuations and transformations, though, one thing does remains constant. Business development, capture, and proposal professionals have strong opinions about and desires for changes that would add sanity and structure to the entire procurement process and cut down on the *guesswork.*

Insights
Capture & Proposal Insights and Tips – Volume 2

I asked a number of my colleagues, "What changes do you anticipate in the next 5 years for the capture/proposal industry, e.g., technology and tools, types of proposals, customers, training, lead time to prepare responses, pricing, etc.?" Here's the second set of their prognostications. How can you and your company begin positioning to address these projected changes?

- The trend toward performance-based contracting will continue to mature as agencies and the companies supporting them gain more experience in this type of contracting. It has been and will continue to be a slow process, because developing, gathering, and evaluating relevant metrics is not a trivial process. Better training in the area of how to identify, track, and evaluate metrics that actually provide insight into the status and quality of a project that explains not only what should be done, but also *how* to do it, would be enormously helpful. *–Margie Regis, Proposal Manager, Management Resources Group and Lohfeld Consulting Group Consultant*

- I expect to see industry pushback that will lead to clearer guidelines on awarding so-called *best value* procurements.
  –Marty Williamson, Proposal Manager and Lohfeld Consulting Group Consultant

- Here are a few industry trends I have observed and expect to continue:

  - Increased level of proposal sophistication (both format and content)

  - More distributed/remote/virtual proposal teams

  - Focus on more sophisticated capture, bid/no-bid, and other pre-RFP processes

  - Heavier use of graphics and increased multimedia for larger, more complex bids

  - Benefit/feature orientation for pricing volumes that includes more proposal themes with supporting narrative and graphics

- Increased reliance on external proposal consultants

  –Chris Simmons, APMP Fellow and Principal, Rainmakerz Consulting

- Very tight DOD budgets, which will mean more competition for small opportunities. Because of this, I think that you will see every eligible vendor under the large IDIQ vehicles bidding as many task orders as possible. Firms that are used to being verbose will have to learn how to compete in the tight (20-page) task order arena.
  –Kristin Pennypacker, Vice President, Proposal & Capture Management, Planned Systems International

- I'm already seeing fixed price contract types for development and sustainment efforts. The top-tier system integrators are accustomed to cost plus contract types for these types of efforts. Evaluation criteria are leaning more toward lowest price technically acceptable, rather than best value to the customer. The government is becoming much more risk averse, transferring more of the cost and schedule risk to the contractors. This means that the contractors must strategize, plan, and estimate differently from what they're used to. *–Pat Cosimano, Owner of Pat Cosimano Wins and Lohfeld Consulting Group Consultant*

- I see less tolerance for any kind of risk and more bundling of contracts into large vehicles. *–Wendy Frieman, APMP Fellow and Principal Consultant, Lohfeld Consulting Group*

- In the next 5 years I expect the following:

  - More formal RFPs from large and small organizations. Expect a greater awareness of the proposal profession as a result.

  - Process and tools will be more critical and more robust due to limited resources.

  - More proposal professionals will be certified. Certification will be expected.

  - Visual communication will play a greater role as competition increases and decision makers' time becomes more fractured.

Insights
Capture & Proposal Insights and Tips – Volume 2

- Capture, sales, and marketing will become more important because they plant the seeds of success.

–Mike Parkinson, APMP Fellow and Principal, 24 Hour Company

21 Experts' predictions for capture and proposal industry changes—Part 3

Beth Wingate

Bundled contracts, unbundled contracts, emphasis on well-trained procurement support staff, training axed in cost-cutting measures, short turnarounds, extended and extended extensions, virtual proposals, everyone in the war room…

The more things change…

Play this government capture and proposal game long enough, and you start recognizing and anticipating the changing patterns. Talk to those who've been in the business for years, and you'll gain insights into how to deal with a particular round of changes based on what the veterans experienced the last go round.

I asked a number of my colleagues, "What changes do you anticipate in the next 5 years for the capture/proposal industry, e.g., technology and tools, types of proposals, customers, training, lead time to prepare responses, pricing, etc.?" Here is the final set of their responses. How will you and your company start positioning yourselves to address these projected changes?

- I expect more bundled contracts with more task orders with short turn around. The government will have to standardize proposals (maybe no past performance questionnaires and all CPARS) to be able to train contracting officers. –*Brooke Crouter, Principal Consultant, Lohfeld Consulting Group*

- The world is getting smaller, and businesses are getting leaner. Over the past decade, the proposal industry has been morphed, re-morphed, and morphed again by revolutionary Internet technology (e.g., webinar capabilities, cloud computing, etc.). As a result, companies are learning the value of virtual proposal writing, and it's taking shape as the norm. I anticipate an even further strengthening of this trend, as businesses continue to reduce overhead by outsourcing proposal needs, using the experts only when needed—and using them virtually to compound savings. *–Luanne Smulsky, Principal, ib4e Writing Solutions*

- The procurement cycle lengthening due to the lack of experienced contracts personnel and the continued issuance of procurements before they are ready for prime time. *–Betsy Blakney, APMP Fellow and Director of Proposal Management, CACI*

- The RFP Dilemma. I believe that our government customers, under increasing austerity pressures, will continue to publish RFPs that remain unclear, eliciting hundreds of questions and resulting in proposals that are difficult to evaluate on merit—resulting in a tendency to award on price. *–Maury Sweetin, Capture Manager/Proposal Manager/Red Team Captain/Volume Lead, Lohfeld Consulting Group*

- The change I anticipate in the next 5 years is that proposals will be paperless, everything will be electronic. *–Mary Beth Frazza, Owner, Frazza Formatting and Lohfeld Consulting Group Consultant*

Insights
Capture & Proposal Insights and Tips – Volume 2

- I look forward to more interactive, customer-focused electronic bids with video and links to reports and web sites with solutions. Bid managers getting involved in capture and solution selling and more customer interaction. More internal focus on bid support from graphics to proposal coordinators and fewer one-man shows! *–Deborah Brooks, Sr. Bid Manager, TATA Communications*

- There is going to be a lot of change. People will become better trained and will have professional accreditations in these fields. Technology abounds and I am always amazed at how few people actually use the tools that are available. Over the next 5 years, we will see broader adoption of tools in both capture and proposals. We will also see better processes, and process measurement will become commonplace. I think in 5 years we will all look back and say how simple things were back then. *–Bob Lohfeld, APMP Fellow and CEO, Lohfeld Consulting Group*

Capture and proposal innovations

Lisa Pafe

With the uncertainties and cost cutting we weathered in previous years, today's market demands contractors increase competitiveness.

An effective way to stop wasting money in a tight market is to increase B&P productivity through innovation. This column addresses innovation across the following areas:

- People
- Processes
- Technology

People

Gone are the days when contractors could afford bloated proposal teams, including high travel costs, three square meals a day plus snacks, and reams of wasted paper. While it may not qualify as an innovation to go lean, our industry has been slow to adopt lean principles such as right sizing. Going lean can be as simple as spending time during the planning stages to assess which types of skills, experience, and competencies—as well as personalities—are needed and when.

Compare what you need to the available pool team-wide, and then don't hesitate to play favorites when selecting the team. Identify and segment each person's competencies and keep track of the same in your database. Just as important as the ability to write might be the ability to collaborate and be a team player.

As the Capture Manager or Proposal Manager, you need to make honest assessments and tough decisions. You can't afford to waste resources by selecting the wrong capture and proposal personnel. Once you have the players identified, cycle them in and out of the team as needed rather than keeping the entire team booked continuously and risking unproductive down time. Not only will this approach reduce costs, but it will also keep the players fresh and focused.

Processes

The best of the breed are eliminating wasteful, multi-step processes and tailoring their approach to leaner times. Innovators ask tough questions. Does it really make sense to ask writers to deliver content and reviewers to review only at set points on the calendar? Should we perform competitive analysis only for Black Hat? Are formal 1- to 2-day color team reviews truly effective?

Innovative companies are borrowing iterative methods from Agile software development. Agile teaches that the longer it takes to find a defect, the more expensive it is to address. Applying the same principle, if we wait until set points on the calendar to perform reviews, recovery will be more difficult.

Smart companies use iterative cycles to respond rapidly to change. They receive and review proposal inputs (competitive analysis, proposal content, review comments) in smaller pieces that the Capture Manager and Proposal Manager deliver to the team in real-time (leveraging technology) to provide immediate feedback. In addition, with the rise in multiple award vehicles and task orders with shorter turnaround times, iterative techniques are more important than ever.

Technology

Enterprise proposal management software is becoming increasingly popular and is proven especially effective for managing and communicating with geographically dispersed and leaner teams. We are all familiar with products that help store, control, revise, distribute, review, and publish proposals through centralized libraries, calendars, search capabilities, and proposal working sites.

Innovations include the trend towards systems that support and enforce specific company capture and proposal processes, automated workflows, and reporting while at the same time integrating, leveraging, and analyzing pipeline information from industry research groups and social media inputs from LinkedIn, Twitter, Facebook, and more.

These integrated enterprise-wide offerings require some upfront investment to define requirements and tailor the COTS offering. However, in the long run, enterprise systems save money, increase collaboration and knowledge transfer, and support continual improvement. The trend towards the cloud and Software as a Service (SaaS) further introduces efficiencies, especially for companies with less mature IT infrastructures.

6 changes experts would make to the business development, capture, and proposal process

Beth Wingate

"Nothing endures but change. Change is the only constant." –Heraclitus of Ephesus

Business transformation, process improvement, continual improvement, business process improvement. Call it what you will. The gist of the matter is that we constantly tinker with the *current state* trying to make it better, faster, more efficient, easier, or more reliable so that we can achieve our desired results.

I asked a number of capture and proposal experts to share their responses to the question, "If you could change one thing about the business development, capture, or proposal life cycle or process, what would that be?"

Insights
Capture & Proposal Insights and Tips – Volume 2

Here are their responses—some eminently achievable, some wonderful end-state aspirations.

- If I were *king,* I would insist that a *yes* bid decision be made only after hardheaded, comprehensive data collection and customer dialog, resulting in a realistic chance to win. There is far too much irrationality in making bid decisions and far too little honest analysis of win probability. To sum up, "Hope is not a legitimate strategy." *–Maury Sweetin, Capture Manager/Proposal Manager/Red Team Captain/Volume Lead, Lohfeld Consulting Group*

- I would emphasize that no proposal best practice can be substituted for a good working relationship with the customer; a knowledge of the customer's business requirements, constraints, and budget tolerance; and an outstanding record of past performance. I would change the misconception that long hours result in a good proposal; actually the opposite is true most of the time. *–Brenda Crist, APMP Fellow and Principal Consultant, Lohfeld Consulting Group*

- Just one thing? As a general statement, I wish procurement [organizations] would act like a machine and not make so many mistakes with timelines, conflicting instructions, and multi-year evaluation processes. My #1 specific change would be no more canceled procurements— especially after a proposal has been submitted. Big waste of money and time. *–Hamid Moinamin, President, Inserso*

- Make communicative, customer-focused graphics. Most graphics I see are made for the author of the graphics and not the decision maker. Most organizations make graphics that are confusing and submitter-centric. The author and proposal submitter are too familiar with the content to see their error and correct it. I recommend a graphics audit or involving a trained conceptualizer (someone trained to turn words and ideas into clear, compelling, winning proposal graphics). *–Mike Parkinson, APMP Fellow and Principal, 24 Hour Company*

- End extensions! They hurt 90% of the time and tend to make the process more difficult, redundant, elongated, and just painful to rearrange schedules. I would also place orals before the written proposal as a down-select tool for the government. Meet the people first, then get the written proposal from those they like. Discussions would follow. *–Ben Rowland, Orals Coach and Lohfeld Consulting Group Consultant*

• The weakness in the proposal process that most concerns me is the development of the *solution*. Often this step is glossed over or skipped completely in the rush to get to Pink Team and start writing. Ideally, all proposals should have a solution that is developed collaboratively between the technical team and the proposal team (including the graphics artist). Often as proposal manager, I have to develop the annotated outline/storyboard with minimal access to the technical team (after all, they have *day jobs*). And, often this access is one-on-one discussions based on a single topic. The result is a compliant outline, but there is no *story*.

This method also leads to inconsistencies as the technical resources who are writing are focused solely on getting their sections done as quickly as possible. What works best is to have a facilitated meeting with all the contributors and the proposal team that walks through the *solution* and decides on the general approach that best responds to the customer's requirements.

The benefit of spending this time (normally about 8 hours depending on the scope and complexity of the requirement) is that the solution is fully integrated, redundancies are eliminated or minimized, the whole team has an overview of the whole proposed solution so they can avoid inconsistencies, and the graphics are fully integrated into the solution and are not dependent on the skills of the individual writers. Time and time again, I have found when I can pull the team together early (before Pink Team) and have them sit in a room together to work through the requirements, the proposal is tighter, more innovative, and easier to write.
–Margie Regis, Proposal Manager, Management Resources Group and Lohfeld Consulting Group Consultant

Insights

Capture & Proposal Insights and Tips – Volume 2

6 more changes experts would make to the business development, capture, and proposal process

Beth Wingate

"He that will not apply new remedies, must expect new evils: for Time is the greatest innovator: and if Time, of course, alters things to the worse, and wisdom and counsel shall not alter them to the better, what shall be the end?" –Francis Bacon

In everything we do in business, we constantly work to make our products, processes, and procedures faster, more efficient, easier, cheaper, or more reliable to gain increased market share.

I asked a number of capture and proposal experts to share their responses to the question, "If you could change one thing about the business development, capture, or proposal life cycle or process, what would that be?"

Here are their responses—some achievable today, others worthy goals requiring increased cooperation between contractors and government/customers.

- I would change the way RFPs are built. I would ask that the government put the same rigor in their process that we put in on our end. *–Brooke Crouter, Principal Consultant, Lohfeld Consulting Group*

- Twenty years ago, the cost of software development was heavily back-end loaded—that is, most funding went into development and test rather than requirements analysis and design. Over time, developers learned that shifting money forward made the final product better. We need to learn that same lesson in terms of B&P funding. If we provide more funding earlier in the cycle, we can better identify programs we should not bid, more effectively influence programs that we should, build better solutions, and improve pWin. *–Randy Richter, President, Richter & Company*

- Responding to RFPs is an inherently inefficient and frustrating process. For the most part, RFPs are poorly written, filled with inconsistencies, generalities, and ambiguities. To make matters worse, the evaluation criteria is often vague, imprecise, confusing, and not aligned with the instructions. These poorly written RFPs result in a significant number of questions, amendments, delays, and even cancellation of bids altogether.

Communication between the end customer and the bidding contractor is generally poor. Instead of passing email messages and documents over an electronic transom, I'd like to see a more open dialogue and meaningful exchange of information between customers and contractors. This approach will have a dramatic effect on the efficiency and effectiveness of both proposal development and proposal evaluation. More importantly, it has the potential to result in solutions that are better aligned with customer needs.

Unfortunately, I don't see this changing in the foreseeable future and would love to hear what others think about how to

improve the communication gap between customers and contractors.
–*Chris Simmons, APMP Fellow and Principal, Rainmakerz Consulting*

- I would like to see even more dialogue between the proposal professionals and the government contracting community. I work exclusively in government contracting and too often see only the business developers and contract managers interacting with the customers. Proposal instructions and the government's intent are often incomprehensible or ambiguous and, as proposal managers, we're often brought in too late to ask clarifying questions that would enable us to outline and implement a clear, well-organized response. Across the various government acquisition activities, there is still a lot of inconsistency in the quality of solicitations from a proposal manager's viewpoint. –*Pat Cosimano, Owner of Pat Cosimano Wins and Lohfeld Consulting Group Consultant*

- It would be nice to see the government standardize more of its solicitations to make it easier for them to convey their intentions and for bidders to understand them. Using more-effective solicitation templates that contain common, unambiguous language would enable government organizations to reduce the number of questions bidders tend to ask over and over. For example, how often do we see the same questions about whether 8 point font can be used for figures, whether a compliance matrix will count against page limits, or a sub-factor appears in the instructions but not the evaluation criteria? Standardized templates that employed more checkboxes, fill-in-the-blanks, and boilerplate text would reduce the amount of time it takes solicitation writers to specify these things, review them, and respond to bidders' questions.

–David C. Hilnbrand, Principal Consultant, DC Proposal Services and Lohfeld Consulting Group Consultant

- There is a tendency to involve too many people in writing and reviewing. I believe that lean teams are more effective.
  –Lisa Pafe, Principal Consultant, Lohfeld Consulting Group

7 more changes experts would make to the business development, capture, and proposal process

Beth Wingate

"The only way to make sense out of change is to plunge into it, move with it, and join the dance." –Alan Watts

In this wrap-up to my 3-part series asking capture and proposal experts to share their responses to the question, "If you could change one thing about the business development, capture, or proposal life cycle or process, what would that be?" my industry colleagues share their practical insights and suggestions.

- I would end the search for the holy grail of a plug-and-play repeatable process for BD, capture, or proposals. Principles apply and rules exist. It's just that for any given opportunity, it might make sense to ignore

or break half of them. –*Wendy Frieman,
APMP Fellow and Principal Consultant,
Lohfeld Consulting Group*

- The proposal process is only as good as its
  leadership. Veteran proposal managers
  demand a smooth process and usually get
  it—building in risk mitigation strategies
  gleaned from lessons learned and
  facilitating efficient, timely problem solving
  for unanticipated issues. While I wouldn't
  necessarily change the process, I would
  recommend it always be led by experienced
  managers. –*Luanne Smulsky, Principal, ib4e
  Writing Solutions and Lohfeld Consulting
  Group Consultant*

- Not holding business developers and
  capture teams accountable for going after
  business they have no business going after.
  Why waste resources when we are all
  trying to do more with less.–*Betsy Blakney,
  APMP Fellow and Director of Proposal
  Management, CACI*

- If I could change one thing about the
  business development/capture/proposal life
  cycle or process, it would be to ensure that
  the schedules and deadlines are respected

and adhered to. Every member of a proposal team—authors, capture managers, proposal managers, coordinators, pricers, graphics, formatters, and editors—has to rely on the others to get their piece of the proposal done in a finite amount of time. If the schedule slips at any level, it impacts the entire team and their ability to get their work done accurately and in a reasonable amount of time. *–Mary Beth Frazza, Owner, Frazza Formatting and Lohfeld Consulting Group Consultant*

- Senior executives need to understand that to develop a capture strategy and develop a compelling and compliant proposal you have to make the investment (time and money). It's not something you can do cheaply—you get what you pay for! *–Kristin Pennypacker, Vice President, Proposal & Capture Management, Planned Systems International*

- The bid qualification process is the one thing I would change. If the sales/capture team has not built a good relationship with the customer, influencing the RFP requirements prior to a bid dropping, there is little chance of winning. Going through the motions of bid qualification and bidding on everything ensures people are overworked on the wrong opportunities. –*Deborah Brooks, Sr. Bid Manager, TATA Communications*

- Every successful company realizes soon or later that it needs to establish repeatable processes for conducting capture and proposal activities. To make these efforts scalable, the company must define and manage new business pursuits using processes that work for them. I have become an evangelist for measuring how well these processes are executed and using these measures to improve process efficiency and effectiveness. If I could change one thing, it would be to get everyone to realize how important it is to establish sound processes and to measure how well the processes are carried out. Measuring the effectiveness of your process is the foundation for optimizing the economic engine of your company. Without measurement, you are just guessing at what needs to be improved. –*Bob Lohfeld, APMP Fellow and CEO, Lohfeld Consulting Group*

Acronym Glossary

Acronym	Definition
APMP	Association of Proposal Management Professionals
B&P	bid and proposals
BD	business development
CMMI	Capture Maturity Model Integration
CO	contracting officer
CONOPS	concept of operations
COR	contracting officer's representative
CO	contracting officer
COTS	commercial-off-the-shelf
CPARS	Contractor Performance Assessment Reporting System
CPI	continuous process improvement
D&B	Dunn & Bradstreet
DCAA	Defense Contract Audit Agency

Insights

Capture & Proposal Insights and Tips – Volume 2

Acronym	Definition
DOD	Department of Defense
DOL	Department of Labor
DOT	Department of Transportation
DTP	desktop publishing
FAR	Federal Acquisition Regulations
FTE	full time employees
G&A	general and administrative
HR	human resources
IDIQ	indefinite delivery, indefinite quantity
IR&D	independent research and development
ISO	International Organization for Standardization
IT	information technology
ITIL	Information Technology Infrastructure Library
JPL	Jet Propulsion Lab
LPTA	lowest price technically acceptable

Insights

Capture & Proposal Insights and Tips – Volume 2

Acronym   Definition

Acronym	Definition
MS	Microsoft
NASA	National Aeronautics and Space Administration
NCA	National Capital Area
NDA	nondisclosure agreement
OCFO	Office of the Chief Financial Officer
ODC	other direct costs
OFPP	Office of Federal Procurement Policy
PDCA	plan, do, check, act
PMBOK	Project Management Body of Knowledge
PMI	Project Management Institute
POC	point of contact
PPIRS	Past Performance Information Retrieval System
PTW	price-to-win
QA	quality assurance
QC	quality control

Insights
Capture & Proposal Insights and Tips – Volume 2

Acronym	Definition
R&D	research and development
RFP	request for proposal
SaaS	software as a service
SB	small business
SF1449	Solicitation/Contract/Order for Commercial Items
SME	subject matter expert
SOP	standard operating procedure
SSB	source selection board
TA	teaming agreement
WBS	work breakdown structure